PRAISE FOR *SANDPAPER SISTERS*

"In *Sandpaper Sisters*, Michele McKnight Baker gives the reader a window through which to view lives in the process of change and restoration. New Life For Girls has been loving, caring, and sharing the love of God with broken people since 1972. It is God alone who gets the glory not only for this book and the story it tells, but also for the countless others whose lives have been made brand new since the inception of this ministry (II Cor 5:17)."

— Jose and Carmela Pacheco
Directors of **New Life for Girls**

"*Sandpaper Sisters* reminds us yet again of the immense power of 'community' to support, nurture, and improve the odds for even those facing the toughest of situations. May the lessons of New Life for Girls inspire us all to become community builders and to surround our children and families with the caring communities they deserve."

—Mrs. Alma Powell
Chair of America's Promise—The Alliance for Youth

"From the first to the last page, Michele Baker captures the reader's attention by thoroughly and compassionately describing the challenging lives of the Life for Girls (NLFG)."

Sandpaper Sisters

Sandpaper Sisters

MICHELE McKNIGHT BAKER, PH.D.

FaithWalk
PUBLISHING
Grand Haven, Michigan

Published by FaithWalk Publishing
Grand Haven, Michigan 49417

Printed in the United States of America
00 09 08 07 06 05   7 6 5 4 3 2 1

Library of Congress Cataloging-in-Publication Data

Baker, Michele McKnight.
 Sandpaper sisters : addicts turned community builders : miracles do happen! / by Michele McKnight Baker.
 p. cm.
 ISBN-13: 978-1-932902-48-8 (pbk. : alk. paper)
 ISBN-10: 1-932902-48-1
 1. Community leadership. 2. Civic leaders. 3. Addicts—Services for. 4. Self-help groups. I. Title.
 HM781.B35 2005
 362.29'185'0973—dc22
  2005015981

DEDICATION

To Frank, a real Proverbs 3 man, with love.

CONTENTS

Part Three
Omega Group and Alumnae

PREFACE

C hances are, someone you care about is an addict. For every substance abuser, there are family members, friends, coworkers, and bystanders who have been damaged by the addiction.

Those of us who are affected keep it hidden, but the statistics confirm that we do not suffer alone. Some 19.5 million Americans over the age of twelve use illegal drugs. More than half of the U.S. population—120 million people—use alcohol; 54 million of these are binge drinkers, while 15.9 million are heavy drinkers. There are no other statistics in this book, so read them here:

•Alcohol- and drug-related cases swamp our courts and prisons; they are the two most prevalent motives for felonies among a record prison population of 6.47 million Americans—1 in 32 adults.

•Substance abuse absents parents from children. The foster/adoptive care system has become a multibillion dollar industry, with more than half-a-million displaced children. Increasing numbers of youth remain in the system and become dependent on social welfare through adulthood.

•A significant correlation exists between substance abuse and homelessness.

•As substance abuse expands, denial ("not my child/ not my community") defeats prevention and early intervention efforts.

•Combating the problem has itself become a multi-billion dollar industry, with over $3 billion spent annually on treatment alone. This does not include related mental and physical healthcare issues.

•The estimated annual social cost of substance abuse in the United States is $276 billion.

The social, economic, and emotional costs of substance abuse pile up and clog multiple systems. This is especially true in cases of women with substance abuse problems.

No wonder the problem of addiction is so often considered hopeless. We choose to abandon the addict or, at best, to fund programs that maintain some semblance of control over them. Most of the residents of the program described in this book represent the "worst of the worst," or "complex cases" to use the clinical term, women with multiple addictions and various psychological and social problems. That is the special power of this story: If *she* can become a community builder, *anyone* can.

Be forewarned: *Sandpaper Sisters* is about lives changed, and it has the potential to change lives. The stories shook my world. I found myself on new and sometimes dangerous ground. In order to write *Sandpaper Sisters*, an adequate storytelling framework could not come just from the social sciences, or religion, or the humanities, but needed to draw from all. Neurologist Oliver Sacks describes his own similar dilemma as a "doubleness" in the Preface to *The Man Who*

Mistook His Wife for a Hat, disclosing that he is "equally if in-adequately both a theorist and a dramatist ... equally drawn to the scientific, and the romantic, and continue to see both in the human condition." He, too, needed to "deepen" the scientific case study, to a "narrative or tale ... only then do we have a 'who' as well as a 'what' ... ."

Sandpaper Sisters is about more than addiction. It is about people. Questions of hopelessness and the impact of individual action coexist with even more profound questions of power, love, community, and relationships. To all of us questioners, these women and men offer up their life journeys and invite us to find, in them, some answers.

—Michele McKnight Baker, 2005

ACKNOWLEDGMENTS

On the winding journey of writing and publishing *Sandpaper Sisters*, it has been my privilege to have the company of some very gifted and special people. I wish to thank Dirk Wierenga of FaithWalk Publishing, who shepherded this project, along with editor Jennifer Phipps, Ginny McFadden and Louann Werksma, a truly supportive community of colleagues.

Words fitly spoken are like apples of gold, as the psalmist says. I am indebted to the timely encouragement of Dr. Mary Pipher, Dr. Tony Campolo, Alma Powell, Dr. Barbara Benedict Bunker, Sherry and Andy Rishel; Sandy, Tom, and Seth Grove; Dr. Janet Avery, Kris Minor, Majors Lurlene and Darren Mudge; Lynne Eib, Karen Hansen, Jack Smith, and members of St. Paul's (Wolf's) Church.

I owe special thanks to the members of the New Life for Girls community who entrusted me with their story, in itself a gracious act of community building.

There is not a section of cheerleaders anywhere in the world more enthusiastic and supportive than my family, with Frank, Andrew, and Dan front and center.

For these blessings and more, thanks be to God: first, last, and always.

INTRODUCTION

New Life for Girls (NLFG) is a faith-based, residential substance abuse treatment program for girls and women aged sixteen and up, its constituency otherwise culturally, ethnically, and socioeconomically diverse. Women enter via one of eight introduction centers in the United States and Latin America, or as referrals from other programs. After three months, they may progress to the main facility, also known as the training center, in Dover, Pennsylvania. Residency typically lasts one year. In recent years, the paperwork to maintain licensure as a treatment program became so burdensome that NLFG leaders decided not to renew. Consequently, NLFG describes itself as a "ministry," not a "treatment program."

New Life was founded in 1972 by Cookie Rodriguez after she graduated from a similar program, Teen Challenge. At the time, few drug treatment programs of any kind existed for women, given their particular psychosocial needs—childcare and recovery from physical and sexual abuse, to name a few. The Puerto Rican-born visionary described her addiction, her treatment, and the founding of NLFG in a book titled *Please Make Me Cry!* (Rodriguez, 1985).

After Rodriguez graduated from Teen Challenge and attended Bible college in the early 1960s, she joined Teen Challenge's staff and attempted to expand its program for women. At first, the focus was on quantity, not quality. In time she came to the conclusion that there needed to be a different approach to treatment for women: "The girls were not responding to the rehabilitation programs in the same way that the fellows were. Despite a stringent screening process, far too many girls were leaving the program prematurely. Among the staff workers, a feeling was growing that girls were too hard to reform. Many were beginning to believe that female junkies were beyond redemption" (Rodriguez, 1985). She and her husband Demi eventually started NLFG with $150 left from their Teen Challenge earnings and enough gifts and loans to make a $10,000 down payment on a 10-acre farm in Dover; it had no habitable buildings. New Life's current directors, Jose and Carmela Pacheco, joined the staff shortly after its founding.

On paper, the NLFG authority structure is elusive to chart. It appears inefficient with redundancies; but, in practice, it works. The day's activities go smoothly, even when the unexpected happens. Residents' job assignments are explicit and in writing, as are descriptions of the various stages of experience, instructions on how to move through the stages, and the rewards and disciplines directly related to progress.

Similar sets of rules and norms apply to both the introduction centers (e.g., Westminster) and the main center (Dover). Life at an introduction center is markedly different from the Dover experience for a variety of reasons: the need for an adjustment period in treatment; rediscovery of emotions; emerging identity traits and capabilities; and so on.

In a nutshell, the resident's life in the smaller community of the introduction center is more structured and cozier than at the main Dover campus. Most of the introduction centers are located in rural or suburban areas, with the exceptions of New York City and Chicago. At both types of centers, there is a posted progress report chart showing what stage each resident has reached, including a listing of who received discipline and what it was. NLFG is designed to be experienced as a residential school, complete with cap-and-gown graduation. The Dean of Women oversees the academic progress of students, including the system of disciplines, with input from teaching and counseling staff. There is not a points-based reward system although there are privileges to which residents may aspire, such as membership in the traveling choir and leadership positions. Whatever enjoyable activities or treats

NLFG has planned are made available to everyone who is not precluded by a discipline.

Throughout the text, all names, with the exception of the author's, have been changed. From time to time the reader will encounter text set in italics, which represents a shift from third-person point of view to the author's first-person thoughts, recollections, and observations. For example:

To tell the stories of the women I met at New Life for Girls with as little distraction as possible, I chose to avoid the academic conventions of superscript numbers and footnotes. When I refer to the studies and works of others within a chapter, the reader who seeks more information may find it in the book's end matter, immediately following the Afterword, in a section entitled "Notes." These source notes and other elaborations are listed by chapter. I hope they are helpful. A vast body of literature informs substance abuse treatment, prevention, and related social issues and so we have intentionally kept references to the necessary minimum. They represent the research and wisdom of just a few of the many authors, social scientiests, and community builders whose work has informed and furthered my own.

PART ONE

A WEEK IN THE LIFE:
WESTMINSTER INTRODUCTION CENTER

*"Let's pretend there's a way of getting through into
it, somehow, Kitty. Let's pretend the glass has got
all soft like gauze, so that we can get through. Why,
it's turning into a sort of mist now, I declare! It'll
be easy enough to get through——." She was up on
the chimney piece while she said this, though she
hardly knew how she had got there. And certainly
the glass was beginning to melt away, just like a
bright silvery mist.*

—Through the Looking Glass

*And it came to pass, as they still went on, and
talked, that, behold, there appeared a chariot of fire,
and horses of fire, and parted them both asunder;
and Elijah went up by a whirlwind into heaven.*

—2 Kings 2:11 (*KJV*)

ONE
WHEN EVERYTHING CHANGED

September, 2001

Brooke

Late on a Saturday night in a drowsy Maryland town, a blonde, 4-year-old girl named J. J. lay awake on her bed, listening for the sound of her mother's voice. The apartment lay quiet now, but earlier it had been full of noise: shouting, first her gramma's voice, then her mamma's; strange voices, too, men ... and the sounds of furniture scraping the floor. She waited until all the noise was gone before she slipped out of bed and into her mother's room. She patted the empty pillow and called softly, but her mother wasn't there. J. J. went back to her room, put on her slippers, and padded into her 2-year-old brother's room.

"Come on, Casey, we're going to go save Mommy."

J. J. told her brother to hold onto the stair railing. She could hear him following her down the dark corridor. When she pushed the door open she felt cold and hugged her arms against her chest. Scary thoughts came to her mind as she walked along the shadowy sidewalk of their street. She tried chasing them away by singing a funny song about pickles. When she got to the corner she realized Casey was not behind her. She could not see him anywhere! She watched the traffic light turn green but hesitated. *Should she look for Casey or cross the street? What would Mommy do? Mommy!* She hurried across the street, car engines roaring in her ears. She saw the bar where her mother liked to go.

She tugged on the sleeve of a man standing near the bar and frowned. "I don't know where my brother is. I came for my mommy. I want to save my mommy!"

When Brooke—J. J's mommy—returned to her empty apartment two days later, she assumed her mother had collected her children. She had no money left. But she knew how to get more cocaine.

Tawanda

The same evening, a gust of wind whipped around the Chicago street corner where Tawanda waited for someone from her crowd to show up. She pulled her coat tighter across her thin shoulders—not that it did much good. Tawanda was always cold, always waiting. Devone had taken the money left from her paycheck and gone to get the liquor. She should have asked him to let her into the apartment first. *Stupid.* Devone seemed okay, she thought, but who could she really trust? They had been together since she left Tom. She refused to stay with a man who beat her. Wouldn't sell her body, either. Years of living on the streets taught her a thing or two about dealing with men. Keep the upper hand. But it wasn't always easy when she was drunk—and she was drunk when Devone met up with her and offered to get the stuff.

Tawanda leaned against the building and closed her eyes. One thought kept surfacing. Her lips barely moved as she spoke it, tapping her head against the wall with every word: "I … am … so … tired."

Rosa

Rosa crawled into the corner of the sofa and lit another cigarette. Her 12-year-old daughter and her mother slept soundly upstairs in their Philadelphia home. She couldn't go back to her girlfriend's apartment. Her jaw still ached from the fight at the dance club. Worse, her heart felt shattered by her girlfriend's betrayal. She couldn't trust men—or women. She would sleep here, maybe do some studying and pull herself together for teaching on Monday. Except that she couldn't sleep. The cravings were bad. And the nightmares had returned. The same dream: She is trapped in a tall burning building, struggling down smoke-filled stairs to find a way out. Her students pass her going up the stairs. Wrong way! She yells, trying to get them to turn around. But they can't hear or see her. She feels the building crumble around her … .

Rosa held her head between her hands and rocked slowly. She felt as if she was losing her mind.

Kenda

The prison guard asked again. Kenda said nothing. Her face was a hardened mask, and her striking green eyes stared straight past the guard. Kenda knew the brawl meant another week in solitary confinement. But she won the fight; that was the important thing. Only the toughest survive. Besides, she told that dyke to keep her hands to herself.

Only after the guard left did Kenda sink onto her cot in despair. How did she wind up here? She was a top student in her Baltimore city school: capable, nobody's fool. She had plans to go to college, medical school perhaps. And she had kept things going at home even when her heroin-addicted mother couldn't—which had become most of the time. Kenda made sure her younger sisters were fed, dressed, and ready for school day after day. Even if her hair wasn't done, she made sure theirs was, until one day when it just got too difficult.

Too many things piled on top of each other. When she used heroin, she could stuff the painful memories. She could forget about the fondling and abuse her stepfather had forced on her all those years. Kenda barely remembered the details of the robbery that ultimately landed her here: felony. Twenty years in prison was forever. There was no hope of ever having a life. She would die here.

Holly

Holly woke up early. It was Sunday morning, she knew that much. Her head felt as if it would split open. A bad hangover. She felt sick and considered going back to sleep. Instead, something made her get up, stumble into the bathroom, and get dressed.

Holly quietly pulled the door closed behind her. Her boyfriend and her 2-year-old son were still sleeping in the apartment. She walked down the street toward the brick church she had passed so many times before. She tried to smooth the wrinkles from her dress, wincing in pain from the pinch of too-small thrift store shoes. She almost turned back half a dozen times, yet she kept walking until she found her way to a seat in the back row of the chapel.

She sat still as everyone around her jumped to their feet, singing and clapping. She thought about her parents and her grandparents worshiping at another church in a nearby town. What a disappointment she had been to them; she never seemed to fit in. Not at school, not at church. Nowhere. Having a baby made her feel like someone for the first time. She loved her son, Bradley, more than anything in the world. Holly rose to her feet and began walking toward the front of the sanctuary to talk to the pastor. It would be almost three months before she saw Bradley again.

Michele

For me, that weekend was like any other. Or so I thought. I had spent all my adult life striving to be the well regarded professional, the well regarded wife and mother, the well regarded Christian.

Oddly, the more I accomplished the more invisible I felt. I am not talking about transparency, because I tend to guard my private thoughts and corral my feelings to keep them from intruding into the arenas of business and academia, which value dispassionate objectivity (particularly in women). I am talking about the opposite of transparency, a state of becoming less knowable to others and to myself. This is invisibility as in blur: constant, busy motion in a partitioned-off life. I had come to a crossroad in my life, just like the women I would soon meet at New Life, and I did not even know it.

On this particular Sunday, I was attending the third day of a seminar in Washington, D.C. I walked from the Metro station to the seminar at a hotel on Rhode Island Avenue NW. On this mild, blue-sky day, D.C. looked beautiful. Out of the corner of my eye I caught the profile of a man swaddled in a worn overcoat and seated in a wheelchair. He was parked on the sidewalk with a cup in hand. It dawned on me that I had passed him on the previous two days and that he must live on this corner, at least during the day. I walked over to him and we began to talk. His name was Paul. We had more in common than I would have guessed. We each had families, we loved to read, and each of us in our own way was on the move. He, too, was invisible, but in a different way. When we parted, both smiling, each of us felt a bit more visible, the conversation better than money in our cups.

I began to wonder about the unconscious "underside" of community inhabited by persons like Paul, those made invisible by homelessness, addiction, or other choices and circumstances that pushed them to the periphery. A few years earlier I had met the directors of a residential substance abuse treatment program for women called New Life for Girls. As I thought about choosing a setting for my doctoral research, New Life inexplicably kept coming to mind.

Though I did not realize it at the time, meeting Paul altered my course, and I ended up navigating the crossroad in my life onto a completely different path from the one I had intended. I had no way of knowing where the path would lead and was unprepared for the unexpected turns along the way.

A few weeks later, at 8:30 on a Monday morning, I headed down a gravel drive toward a white farmhouse in Westminster, Maryland. My suitcase shifted in the trunk. Two women emptying garbage cans into a dumpster paused to stare at me. I stared back as I parked. Months of planning had preceded this day; it was too late to back out now. I would spend the next week living here as part of my doctoral research in organizational studies, to observe in depth an organization that was also a community. Only the two directors knew about my research plans. To everyone else I would be just another addict beginning a recovery program.

The two women dragged the empty cans back into the house.

I felt like Lewis Carroll's Alice, entering an entirely different world and not at all prepared for it. Instead of disappearing down a rabbit hole, however, I was stepping into a house in which eighteen strangers lived, including Brooke, Tawanda, Rosa, Kenda, and Holly.

I sat in my car and studied the house. With plain white siding, it rose three stories, capped at the front by a Victorian-style cupola and at the far side by a brick chimney. A banner strung overhead bore the logo and name of the program—New Life for Girls. The yard and adjacent buildings had a well used yet tidy appearance. Bare paths in the grass threaded toward clean-swept paved areas.

What happened inside those walls? Was I at risk? I knew this was a Christian program and that it was "tough"—whatever that meant. I wondered which of the eleven windows I could see would frame my view of the world for the next week.

I glanced at my watch, gathered my papers and belongings from the front seat, then slipped out of the car and locked it. After pulling my suitcase out of the trunk, I took my time walking up the steps to the front door.

TWO
DOWN THE RABBIT HOLE

Monday, September 24, 2001

*T*he house is buzzing with activity, everyone engaged in some sort
of cleaning chore. Geena, a staff member, meets me—the newest
resident—and goes through my belongings. She takes the contents of
my purse,, including my money, ID, penknife, aspirin ("We don't
know for sure what it is."), keys, book ("We don't know its contents.") pepper spray, pictures ("You may have family pictures, no pictures of boyfriends."). She lists everything and puts them in a plastic
bag to give to Dennis, the staff member who will be my counselor. I
pay the $50 entry fee by check. That is the only fee charged for this
year-long residential program.

Nine women stand around outside the locked classroom waiting for the teacher, who is also the center director, to show up.
It's a mild fall day—sweater weather. The leaves of the mature
trees that ring the property are just beginning to add their
colors to a vivid blue sky. An auburn-haired woman named
Tristes speaks to the new resident in Spanish. When the newcomer responds in Spanish, Tristes grins broadly and begins
speaking, rapid-fire. Tristes wants to know about her, where
she is from, if she has children. The other woman responds in
elementary Spanish.

The director bounds up to the group, a dimpled Cheshire-
cat grin on his round face. He unlocks the door, and the
women follow him into a classroom with a central aisle and
tables on each side.

The class topic is "Jesus is the High Priest." Some of the
women take notes and look up Bible verses. The director

knows his audience. He is a perceptive teacher, sensing what people need to hear; they respond to him. At one point an ash blonde named Brooke, in tears, says, "You are saying exactly what I'm feeling."

At 10:30 a.m., the director closes his Bible and yields the podium to a strict-looking staff member named Chere. She says, simply, "Prayer time." Chairs clatter as all the women kneel. They pray for half an hour on their knees.

Some pray silently, some in low-toned whispers. Chere goes from woman to woman, praying for each of them. Several women moan, some say words of agreement, and others cry. Chere announces the end of prayer time and the beginning of chapel. Time has passed quickly, and people feel refreshed.

Chapel consists of singing and a form of acknowledgements called "God bless you's." A somber, umber-haired young woman named Kenda stands and looks in the direction of the new resident. She says, "I want to bless Michele because I know what it feels like to be the new person. I want Michele to feel welcome."

After chapel is a rest period until lunch. Those who return to their rooms are not allowed to lie down on their beds. The new resident is introduced to her roommates, Tawanda and Sheila, and her bed, an upper bunk above Tawanda, in a dorm-style bedroom named "Kindness." There are two other bedrooms for residents, "Joy" and "Peace."

During the rest period, several of the women head to the living room to lounge and talk.

Tawanda is one of them. She is a tall, slender woman with curly, dark hair and an unlined face the color of milk chocolate. Her front teeth are missing. She has a glib sense of humor and is comfortable pulling others into conversation. Listening to Tawanda requires concentration: Her speech consists of slangy observations delivered in a contralto voice. Her drawl darts from loud to soft swiftly, and often she is asked to repeat herself. She sizes up Michele with a squint and decides to take her under her wing.

"Kenda done blessed you, didn't she Michele? That's nice. Where'd you say you was from again? Pennsylvania. I never been to Pennsylvania. Say, what kind of food you like? I can cook! Yes, girl. Umhmm. that's right. My turn to cook is coming up. Gonna have me a restaurant some day, that's right."

Another woman, Sheila, tosses her brassy brown waves of hair, laughing. She has faint scarring around her neck, the type that suggests she was badly burned at one time. There is a gap between her front teeth. She has a tentative, sweet voice—a girl's voice—and likes to show pictures of her children. Sheila has three young children, an infant girl and two boys. They are dark while she is pale. She talks a bit about growing up in an urban neighborhood, making it clear that she feels more a part of black culture than her own.

Showing pictures of one's children is a favorite getting-to-know-you ritual. Brooke looks at Sheila's photos and runs to her room for hers. She shows Sheila a picture of her daughter, with long blonde hair and huge eyes, a mirror image of her cheerleader-pretty mother. Her son is blonde, too, his features less distinct in the snapshot. She talks about her children: "J. J.—that's short for Jennifer Jasmine—will be five soon. Casey's two." She smiles shyly, beginning to say something else, when Chere announces that it is time for lunch.

The women line up single file in a dining area next to the kitchen. Much of the food is donated. The residents call the donations "blessings." There is an oddball variety to the selection of beverages and side dishes, which includes flavored soymilk, pink cookies, and yogurt-flavored dessert bars.

The women must ask permission to do most everything: to enter the kitchen, leave the dining room, or go outside. Staffers on duty know where they are at all times. After lunch the group drifts outside. They must stay on one side of an outbuilding, where wrought-iron chairs and a table sit in a patch of shade under an oak tree. The men in the new men's program are using the yard and picnic table seating on the other side of the building.

Another new woman has arrived, Rosa. She does not join in any activities. Rosa is Spanish-speaking. Part-time staffers Daniella and Maria are bilingual (Spanish/English). The part-time staff are also in the process of completing the treatment program.

Of the six full-time staff, two couples are bilingual.

Maria, one of the part-time staffers, offers to take the women for a walk. On this day the sky is overcast, threatening rain. A lovely breeze, not too cool, quickens their step. Though Route 140 is a busy street, the side street is a quiet country lane. Gravel and dirt with tufts of grass spring from the rutted shoulders. They talk and walk in changing pairs and threesomes, in no particular or fixed grouping; it's relaxed and informal. They walk past a graveyard, two farmhouses, and a cornfield.

Maria is originally from Mexico. She lived in Chicago while attending a university prior to coming here. Maria has an animated round face and a boisterous laugh. She talks about her mother and how she misses her good home cooking. Then she talks a bit about college life, mentioning her drug use in passing; she is quick to explain that talking about "using" is against the rules.

Maria identifies where the others are from: Tawanda, Chicago; Holly, Brooke, and Mona, suburban Maryland; and Sheila, a small town in Pennsylvania. Tristes and Rosa, the newest resident, come from Philadelphia. Both are Puerto Rican. Tristes came through Philadelphia briefly to see her college-age son and her sister who lives there—and to get clean—while Rosa has lived in Philadelphia from childhood. Kenda is from Baltimore, same as Chere. Geena is from New Jersey.

On the way back from the walk it begins to rain. Everyone lingers outside on the porch as long as they can, until the wind blows the rain in their faces. Then they move to the living room and continue sharing stories. No staff member is there.

Brooke breaks into a conversation saying: "You talking about prison? Uh, it's so boring."

Tawanda responds: "I never been to prison. Been to jail a few times. One time," she chuckles, "I was so drunk I couldn't remember my social security number." She slaps her thigh. "So they kept me in jail overnight. Oh, I cried!" Now she laughs as she retells it; her listeners are laughing, too.

Michele naively asks, "Jail is different from prison?"

Tawanda narrows her eyes at her. "Girl, don't you know the difference between jail and prison? Jail's overnight. Prison's a loooooong time."

Kenda grunts in disdain. "All the starch they serve you in prison. Snack foods. And nothing to do! You couldn't go outside. We were locked into these little dormitory cells, and you either slept, watched TV, wrote, read, or did hair—that's mainly what I did. That's how I got so big. Laying around eating all day. You can go crazy in that place!"

Brooke agrees, "I spent so much time in bed, it just made me all the more tired."

Kenda stares at a spot on the carpet, her memories transporting her to another place. She speaks so softly, few of the women can clearly hear her. "There's a lot of drama that goes on in jail, a lot of chaos. You're just surrounded by it, 24/7. You're just trying to stay away from the crazy women and stay away from the lesbians, and not get mixed up in that type of group. It's hard being in, it's hard to keep to yourself; you try to, but you're in there and there's nothing else to do. Keeping to yourself will get you depressed. You're going to think about yourself and everything that's going on, think about going

home, so you interact with people, but you try to choose
certain groups that you want to hang with. They have cliques
in jail, and you try to be with the clique that's going to get
the most respect."

At 5:00 p.m. the group breaks for dinner, which consists
of green beans, chili, rice, gravy, and dessert. Kenda, tonight's
cook, gets many compliments for the rice. The women are
required to wait for the staffer on duty to say "it's over" before clearing their plates to the kitchen. There is even a well
rehearsed ritual for cleaning the dishes: scraping them over
the garbage can, rinsing them at the sink, handing them to
residents who will wash them.

After dinner, showers begin. Residents have only ten minutes total bathroom time, and showers may not last longer
than seven minutes. Some residents tease Michele for fretting
over the time. While waiting, the women sit in the hallway on
the stair steps between the bedrooms and the bathroom. Holly,
Maria, and Tristes are talking. With Maria translating, Tristes
explains in Spanish that she grew up in a Catholic family. She
has spent seventeen years on drugs, mainly cocaine and crack,
and has been through two marriages. Her family has always
been supportive and never condemning, Now she has a 60-
year-old boyfriend (twenty years older than she) who is a
Christian. He is waiting for her back in Puerto Rico.

Tristes teaches the others a simple song that pairs words
in both Spanish and English. She talks about Jesus as cordero
(lamb) and pastor (shepherd). Now six women have gathered in the hallway, studying for final exams while they wait.
Soothing strains of Celtic psalms music drift from Emily's
room. Maria keeps an eye on the time as women file in and
out of the bathroom.

Rules are posted on a bulletin board outside the bath-
rooms. Actually, two sets of rules, titled (in perplexing Wonderland style) "House Rules" and "More Rules." There are
more than thirty of them. They include the number of items

allowed in the bedrooms and where they are to be placed (two clothing items per person … ; bookshelves are for books only), general rules (sleep between sheets and not on top of blankets … ; underwear must be hand washed), rules of behavior (no gossiping, no touching), and schedule rules (no talking after lights out, no one allowed on beds until after 5:00 p.m.).

The rules are born of street smarts and are proven to work. . Many women have difficulty with the "no touching" and the "no talking about the past" rules. (Later, someone clarifies that it means just the addiction part, not the whole past.) The rules are designed to replace old behaviors and habits with new behaviors, but they have the potential to cut out an enormous part of human interaction. There are often long periods of silence among the residents. Some women break the silence with praise songs. There is much discussion of class material, and God-talk.

After shower time the women make their way down to the kitchen, pajama-clad, for study hall at 8:00 p.m. Chere strictly enforces the no-talking rule during study hall. After a grace period of two weeks called "blackout," new residents are subject to the disciplines for rules-breaking. The rules apply to all residents. A discipline can range from writing a paper, to losing free time privileges and performing extra jobs, to having time added to their stay in the introductory phase.

During study time everyone works with intensity. The mood is not the giggling, cramming study-fests of high school. These women are after something and they are not giggly schoolgirls. The quiet wraps around the group like a blanket, though not oppressive. I study the women's faces, read their glances at each other, notice who sits with whom. Tristes catches me looking and smiles. Her reddish brown hair falls over her shoulders in tight waves. Kenda wears her aloof mask tonight. Her moods alternate between a spontaneous, almost child-like affection and a distance so chilling that the total effect throws an

invisible wall around her. She has a Cleopatra face, emerald eyes in a
darkly regal setting—an African princess. I sense her loneliness.

After an hour Maria calls the women into the living room for
devotions. She settles into the armchair, a smiling big sister.
She seems least like staff, most like a resident.

Some sit on the sofas, some on the floor. Maria reads a
passage of Scripture about having the power to move mountains by faith. "Jesus says, 'If you have faith as small as a mustard
seed, you can say to this mountain, "Move from here to there"
and it will be moved. Nothing will be impossible for you'"
(Matthew 17:20). She asks, "What are your mountains?"

Holly speaks first. What she has to say is so heartbreaking
one would expect her doe-brown eyes to fill with tears, but
they do not. None of the women cry over their own stories.
Holly punctuates her sentences with the soft, southern drawl
of the Maryland region and an apologetic little laugh.

"You guys could pray for me and my son Bradley. I really
miss him. It's hard you know—he's so little. He doesn't understand what's going on. I know he misses me. He's with my
parents, I know they take good care of him and all, but he has
a lot of energy. They're old … " her voice trails off. "It's hard
for me to talk about personal stuff. I'm pretty quiet, guess you
noticed that." The others join her nervous laugh.

"It's hard you know, to trust. Hard for me to trust men. I
really thought my boyfriend loved me. But he's, I don't know,
he's kind of selfish. And lazy. He wanted me to have an abortion. I couldn't do that. He just wants the sex and stuff. I know
now he doesn't treat me right. He couldn't take care of Bradley by himself so … " She shifts weight shyly, dimples appear-
ing at her elbows. She has long curly hair with straight-across
bangs and a faint crescent of freckles. To some she might re-
semble a Campbell's Soup kid, all grown up.

"I know my parents are disappointed in me. I really let
them down. They've gone to church all their lives, sent me to

church camp and stuff like that, and here I am. They don't say they're ashamed of me, but I can see it in their eyes. That real hurt look, you know?"

She opens her Bible to a bookmarked page. "Anyway here's my favorite verse." She reads the words of Old Testament prophet Jeremiah: "'For I know the plans I have for you' declares the Lord, 'plans to prosper you and not to harm you, plans to give you hope and a future'" (Jeremiah 29:11).

Every woman has something to say. Nearly all follow the pattern Holly has modeled, telling fragments of stories from their past (which is permitted during devotions), and concluding with a favorite Bible verse. A number of references are from the Old Testament prophets. It is as if they are prophesying into their own lives hope, power, and a radically different future.

Most of the women mention lacking self-esteem. Rosa admits to having "cravings," and it is clear she is having a hard time. She sits on the floor and stares at the rug, sullen; she is rocking slightly, her dark, spare form making sharp points. Avian, a bird on a wire. Earlier she showed the women a picture of her daughter and mother (all three have the same cascade of dark hair and earnest features) with a terse commentary: "They are both Christians."

Rosa alternates among emotions ranging from contempt for the group ("I don't belong here with you people."), to fear and anxiety ("This is not what I expected."), to apologies ("I will try to be more positive.").

Devotions conclude with prayer offered by Maria, who remembers each woman and her expressed needs, and the women disperse to their bedrooms. Michele uses the makeshift ladder of the bedframe to climb into her upper berth. Sheila and Tawanda engage her in bedtime chatter. They rehash the day, laughing over someone's comments or antics. A rumor is circulating that someone is leaving. (Who could it be?) Before long Maria comes to the door and asks Tawanda to pray for the room. She flicks the light switch, and the room goes dark. Lights out, no talking.

In the darkness I can make out the worn edges of mismatched furnishings in our tidy dorm room. From the upper bunk I can also see faint stains, a patchwork of repairs, and, in the corners, trails of previous layers of paint.

Soon the regular breathing turns to gentle snoring coming from the vicinity of Sheila's bed. The whole house is a quiet cocoon. Everyone falls asleep listening to the silence.

THREE
ALICE IN THE MIRROR

Tuesday, September 25, 2001

A staffer named Shantay does wakeup call. We are awakened late and have to hurry through our turns at the bathroom "Three minutes per person! Soap your face while you're waiting, use the toilet, brush your teeth, and that's it!" The ladies find a tactful way to let me know I am going out of turn ("You're after Tristes, Michele."). Turns are in order of arrival, so the newest resident (Rosa) is last. This is true of the meal line, too. The pecking order, a sort of seniority, operates in a lot of situations here.

With so little time for dressing, makeup, and hair, the residents are au naturel, for the most part. Most of them have almost no time for anything but the basics. The low-maintenance routine leaves residents feeling vulnerable and unattractive; they wear their hard lives on their faces. Every woman in the program shows some sign of physical damage: scars, yellowed or missing teeth. It's not necessarily a bad thing to wear scars, someone observes. Jesus had them. But scarring on the face is hard for people—women especially—to handle. Sheila's face shows evidence of burning. She talks about her stepmom pouring scalding bathwater on her when she was four or five. The residents look for scars on newcomers.

Holly notes, "We all have scars. Some of them show and some of them don't."

Breakfast consists of coffee cake, cereal, and peaches. Food comes daily from different contribution sources. Dropped-off donations are called "blessings" and the residents mobilize to sort and store them. Chere scolds her daughter for mimicking her. "Line up ladies," the little girl chirps. Staff children are a regular part of the household scene. And, though they have the benefit of experiencing new people and situations, the children sometimes use the fact that they have privileges that the adult residents don't have to demean them.

After breakfast everyone has assigned chores. Chere shows the new residents how to do their jobs. In the living room, for example, someone wipes everything from furniture to walls with a disinfecting solution in a bucket. The TV and entertainment center glass gleam from Windex; vacuuming is also part of the job. Residents must ask staff to check their chores at each stage and on completion, and must also seek permission to cross from the hall to the reception area where most of the supplies are stored. There is also a bedroom chore for each resident. New residents, not accustomed to such structure, find it challenging. The routine is complex, and each day has a separate schedule.

The classroom door is unlocked, but the teacher has not arrived. While waiting for the morning class to start, some women discuss "breakdowns," a form of studying at the main campus in Dover (the next phase of the program) during which a dictionary and a concordance are used to break a Bible verse down into the meanings of each word (Greek, English, and biblical contexts).

When Chere arrives to teach "Successful Christian Living," she spends the first fifteen minutes or so transcribing notes to the white board as the women dutifully write them down. Then she explicates. As part of the teaching, she shares information about her life and her testimony. She mentions that she is a hairstylist and at one time owned her own shop. Chere's precisely layered short burgundy brown hair and her meticulous makeup and nail polish are evidence of her craft.

She says, "I went through all the sins listed in Galatians 15:19–21—and then some. I attended the Rock Church, where parishioners spoke in tongues. My grandmother spoke in tongues. It sounded silly to me, like gibberish. Yet I wanted to know God, I just didn't know how. In church, I prayed to know that the tongues were real." She gazes at the ceiling, remembering. "I felt a sensation, like a hand on my back. I felt overwhelmed with joy. And I began to speak in tongues." This is her sixth time back in the program, Chere explains, including the two times she was kicked out. Her downfalls: going back to live with her mother ("an enabler") and cigarettes.

At break, Rosa says, emphatically, "This is not the place for me. It's okay for you to be Christians, but it's not for me." She leaves the room upset. Many assume she will not be back. After break and the half hour of prayer, the men join the female residents. They sit on one side of the room, and the women sit on the other.

Everyone has gathered together to hear a guest speaker, a pastor from Thailand. Born into a Buddhist family, he became a Christian at age fifteen. He encourages listeners to look beyond their own lives and serve the world around them. As the memory verse for Chere's class puts it, " ... but ye shall receive power, after that the Holy Ghost is come upon you; and ye shall be witnesses unto me both in Jerusalem, and in all Judea, and in Samaria, and unto the uttermost part of the earth" (Acts 1:8, KJV).

The women are surprised and relieved when Rosa returns after lunchtime. Before entering the program she was an assistant teacher in a preschool progam; she wants to finish her bachelor's degree in early childhood development. The women sit outside and study after lunch cleanup. Tawanda and Holly, along with Chere's 4-year-old daughter Patty, sit on the couch. Tawanda and Holly try to read, while Patty pretends to be a lion. Then Patty drapes her jacket over Tawanda's head and asks her to be "the grandma." Tawanda acts up a storm; she's hilarious, witty in her street-colloquial way. Patty draws the others into her fantasy.

"There's a mouse behind the sofa!"

"No, child, there's no mouse," Tawanda says, amused.

"Yes, look for yourself!"

Tawanda throws herself over the back of the sofa melodramatically and glances around. She gasps. "Sure enough! I sees that little critter."

"Here." The pink tip of Patty's tongue emerges in concentration. She gathers the ends of the scarf over Tawanda's head and folds them into a knot, transforming her into a granny.

"I know who will get the mouse. Here comes the wolf. But you better watch out, Granny!"

Tawanda makes a delightfully frantic Granny. Holly can't contain her laughter.

All residents are expected to serve in the choir. During the afternoon choir rehearsal, Patty and her brother provide an enthusiastic audience for the songs. The choir is practicing for a special twentieth anniversary banquet and fundraiser on Friday. The banquet has changed the rhythm of the week. Residents are excited and hope family members will come. Camila, the choir director, opens the door to catch an afternoon breeze. Residents can see blue sky and an apple tree, symbols of freedom.

The dynamics of the New Life community emerge. Superficially, the rules create a framework, a structure for behavior and culture formation. Of course, residents pay close attention to what staff does, not just what they say. For example, the rules "When in doubt, ask the staff," and, "No student should tell another student what to do" create a culture in which help comes from peers in small, secretive increments; but all must wait for larger approval or assurance from staff. If a discipline has been meted out for infractions, residents become less willing to answer one another's questions. Residents spend a lot of time waiting. There are silences that seem to be a part of discipline, which is private. So, for example, Sheila is not permitted to talk to Mona or Kenda today. Sheila refers to it tangentially, with no explanation. Kenda did not complete her kitchen duty and is sulking. Secrets. Yet the atmosphere is not oppressive. On the contrary, Brooke describes the place as feeling "safe," compared with two other program experiences she has had, Alcoholics Anonymous and a shorter-term secular residential program.

Most of the staff are alumni and have important information to share. They draw from their experience as do the residents. They lead by example in parenting, lifestyle, and daily choices. They show emotion at times; it is still close to the surface. In class, Chere mentioned having dreams about chasing drugs. "The devil thinks that will put me farther from God, but actually it just makes me sicker of drugs."

Personalities emerge. Tawanda has leadership qualities, including her sense of humor, tact, and a strong sense of responsibility for herself and the other women. She almost graduated from NLFG once before but was caught smoking. She has a maternal affection for the younger women.

Mona has also been partially through the program before. She got a perfect score on her last test, though she describes herself as a "slow student" who did not like school. Kenda, to whom studying comes easily, encourages her. Kenda also has leadership qualities.

At dinner, Kenda smiles mischievously and tells a revealing story. "I enjoyed high school, but in my favorite class, journalism, I didn't like the teacher so I skipped the class for most of the year. Then they told me I couldn't graduate without passing the class, so I crammed and passed.

"I went to college." Kenda looks at her dinner plate as she talks, jabbing at a mound of Jell-O with her fork. "But first I went in the Army. Came home after basic training because I was diagnosed with asthma. Went to college, then withdrew because I was using heroin. Withdrew, not kicked out or dropped out, because I had grades. If you are kicked out or dropped out, you can't get any grades when you decide to go back. I withdrew, so once I go back I can get those grades."

Sheila nods. "That's smart. Hey, when I was in high school, I was failing, girl. One time I used that white-out stuff to change the grades. When my folks found out, they thought it was funny." She snickers, remembering. "Anyway, I didn't like school at all."

It is prayer time. Sheila volunteers to pray first. Maria praises Holly for her gift of hospitality, and it is true: Her sweet smile and gentle spirit are welcoming. Tristes also has a gentle and caring manner. She expresses concern for Kenda, Rosa, or whomever she sees hurting. She is older and more conservative than the others. For example, she is alarmed when she overhears Rosa make a veiled reference in Spanish to being gay. Tristes often doesn't understand what is said in English, and she can be easily bruised. She loves to talk, unlike Brooke, who has a quiet spirit. Brooke wears a cross, a gift from her mother that contains her birthstones.

This evening a new woman arrives. She is put in the large room called "Peace." Accepting almost constant change is not easy, and it's not the normal response of groups. But it's a fact of life here. It's evidence of what this community would call Holy Spirit power.

The newcomer, Lucille, is now the low woman on the totem pole. When she takes her shower out of turn, Tawanda, Rosa, and others protest. She and the other newcomers must wear dresses during this initial two weeks of "grace," a period that permits newbies to learn the rules without penalty. Pants are not allowed until after this phase (called Genesis) is over. Other privileges kick in at different stages.

Later that night the women gather in the living room for devotions. Tristes (with Rosa translating) describes her bad dreams prior to coming here. She notes that there are no bad dreams here. Someone seconds that—and begins to cry. The emotions take everyone by surprise. These women's stories represent so much untapped potential.

FOUR
UNSPOKEN DREAMS

Wednesday, September 26, 2001

The director calls me out of prayer time to talk to him in his office. The walls are lined with shelves brimming with books and photos. I am thinking about how I will disclose my researcher role to the women. I tell the director I want to honor the trust they have placed in me. His response: "You realize, Michele, that you would not be here if we had any doubts about the wisdom and safety of it." He adds, "Save it for Sunday." He says he will have the group pray for me then.

Chere teaches the class called "Trusting God." Everyone seems to appreciate her ability to draw from personal experience—and her transparency. She is surprised by the compliments.

She illustrates her points by using examples from her life. Chere tells the story of her mother, who urged her to "cry out for the blood of Jesus" to protect and deliver her. She also offers her own life as the definition of debauchery: "Dissipated—that was me. I had a drug-induced heart attack. My life was so wasted that death would have been a pleasure. I was too chicken to take my own life. One day when I was on the streets I was startled by my reflection in the windows—just sickened by the sight. I had to look away." She steadies her voice before continuing. "When I looked again, I saw Jesus walking with me. God delivered me from that hell."

Chere glances around the classroom. "You all know what I mean by hoppers." Heads nod. "Kids raised in the projects. From infancy, they're hardened by survival. We are raised in a material world and are need-oriented. It is a world without hope. Hoppers have nothing." She pauses to find a passage in her Bible. "Sometimes God tears things down to build them back up."

The New Life director's and staff members' job duties are many and the compensation is low. For example, each staff member has a counseling role as well as maintenance and administrative duties. One counselor, Dennis, has his own maintenance and cleaning business, which helps his wife and him to afford to remain on staff at New Life while supporting their young family. He was in the investment field prior to working for New Life.

"I know what it's like to have a nice paycheck," he says, smiling. "The paycheck is definitely not why I am here." In working for NLFG, he chooses not to focus on material things. Substance abuse was not part of his background, though it was for a first wife who left him and their children after they relocated to this area with her parents. He ended up living with his estranged wife's family. "I did what I had to do. I am a survivor." Self-reliance was his challenge. The director met him when he was a Mormon, and they developed a relationship. After Dennis became a Christian the director invited him to work for NLFG. That is when he met his current wife, Camila, who is also on staff.

Dennis invites me to sit on the back porch with him and talk. He has a gentle but matter-of-fact way. I tell him what I am learning about myself, mentioning the "mountain moving" discussion from evening devotions. Just as I did with the director, I express my concern that the trust of the women be honored in my conversation with them. He has a different view from the director, and thinks it might be better to discuss my research role and departure during a regularly scheduled Saturday group meeting. He is in agreement on one point that the director emphasized: Don't try to plan it out, but let the Holy Spirit lead. I am a planner by nature; that will not come easily to me.

This is not a typical counseling session: It would be hard to replicate the way counseling plays out for the residents. I have to think about how to explore that. As we talk, I notice some nonverbal cues. He seems a bit uncomfortable at first, and I gather from his questions that he wonders whether I am evaluating his effectiveness as a counselor. I take time to explain my research intentions in some detail, which seems to reassure him. Dennis does not offer much eye contact but seems sincere when he does. There are others here who give little eye contact—Kenda, Mona, and Lucille in particular. I definitely perceive those who do provide eye contact as being more honest, genuinely open, and trustworthy. I catch myself on that last word: trustworthy. I have considered how and whether I am earning my fellow residents' trust, and, yes, they are earning my trust in specific ways.

The culture at New Life is open, surprisingly so, given how protective staffers are of the women. The problem of a closed culture, of course, is that it perpetuates dual lies: There is no hope and no escape. That is why voluntary participation is so important; otherwise any program (or religion) just substitutes one lie for another. New Life consistently turns down government funding because it would require compromise regarding their faith-based approach, and, ironically, the voluntary admission.

Today everyone is at loose ends because Mona was asked to leave due to problems with attachment and manipulation. The newest woman, Lucille, is particularly anxious about whether it was Mona's choice.

It is a fasting day; the women skip lunch and have dinner at five, so they have more free time to study or relax. As Tawanda sits in the living room she recalls how she learned the blues and sang them when she was drinking. Later she learned gospel music. She talks about her family and early childhood. "I have six sisters—there are seven of us girls altogether now. Both my parents are deceased. They died at a very young age. Both were alcoholics. My mother died from lung problems, tuberculosis. Back then they didn't have nothing for it. And my father was murdered, killed in his sleep. My aunt who raised me died when she was eighty-something. Lung problems, too. I'm forty."

As if just realizing it, Tawanda says, "My mom's been dead thirty years." Her expression changes to sadness. "I lived with my aunt since day one. See, that's where the rejection comes in. We was talking about that before? Rejection. I never fit in nowhere. My mom had kids after me. But she didn't give them away, see what I'm saying? Every relationship I had, I was good enough for a certain period of time. I took rejection and replaced it with drugs, alcohol, men. I always had the sense that what one man wouldn't do for me another man would.

"My aunt really loved me," she exclaims. "Oh man, she spoiled me rotten, she did. I had the best: a Shetland pony, a squirrel monkey named Chico. We kept the pony in the suburbs. My uncle would come get me on the weekends, to spend weekends with him. And I don't call him my uncle—I call him daddy still. He's all I've known as a father. My real daddy, even though he was a winehead, loved me. He used to babysit me. He was funny, like me. He used to love to dance, and sing, and play his guitar. I thought he was everything, you know? When they told me he died, it hurt me so. He didn't want to give me away, I don't think. He used to come over and spend weekends. He would call my mom and say, 'I want to come spend time with Tawanda.' Well, he had tuberculosis, gave it to my mother. My aunt didn't want him around me; he used to tell me he was my real daddy. My uncle would say, 'Don't tell her that.' Then the divorce between my aunt and uncle happened and everything came out. I was ten—yeah, that's when it all came out: That's your sister, that's your cousin, that's your daddy."

Tawanda squirms uncomfortably on the sofa. "It was confusing. I remember one time my aunt put her gun on the table because she thought my mother was coming to get me. She was going to shoot; my aunt was going to kill my mother.

You can ask my sisters. During the divorce, the judge asked me who I wanted to live with, my uncle or my aunt. There was a whole bunch of commotion; I decided to stay with my aunt.

"I've always preferred hanging out with men. You know why? Because I knew I wouldn't be rejected. Men are easier to get along with than women, especially on the street. Even though they want something, it's easy to deceive them; they're not quite there yet. Especially on the street. The men I went around with, they never let me get hurt—just tried to get in my pants. But I could easily manipulate them. Basically it was just me and these guys.

"During high school, the boys liked me because I could dance! They wanted to look good on the floor with a certain dance we would do called steppin'. And I would dress smack daddy down." Tawanda throws her head back, laughing. "The other girls was all lacy-like, with high heels; I had steppers, low heels like men's spectator shoes, and pointy toes. I got the foot for it and I got the height; I would put on the suit, the pantsuit, go out there with my megaphone, and step—I would STEP!" She hops to her feet and does a step or two. She glows with pride, remembering.

"In my day just the guys used to do it, and it was hard to teach a girl how to turn. You have to turn a certain way, you got to drop dip and twist your body a certain way." She moves through the step as she talks. "Some girls can do it now, they was bopping, but when it came to steppin', guys would step with guys. I'm a good dancer, just like my dad.

"I didn't start drinking until my sixteenth birthday, and then I didn't drink no more until I got to seventeen. When my aunt found out she gave me a what for and a how to get there." Tawanda laughs. "If I drank I would make sure I just had a bitty drink, just for the fellowship. I got to twelfth grade; all I had to do was go to summer school and make some credits up. Didn't go." Tawanda sighs and sinks back onto the sofa.

"That was my auntie's dream, for me to get my diploma. That's one thing about coming to this program, I really want to get my education. That woman was good to me. She spoiled me, but she believed in God and knew how to raise me. I got rebellious because I wanted to be part of my sisters' life, so that's where all the trashing and division came between me and her. When my mother died, I told her I wanted my mother back, she told me she was my momma. I said no, you're not. And I regret that, because it was uncalled for." She begins to cry softly.

Tawanda gathers herself and changes the subject to talk about New Life. She admits the humiliation of having to enter the program a second time after coming within four months of finishing. "Anger got me sent back all the way." Because of the phases of the program, she now is subject to the authority of staff members who were once residents under her former junior staff leadership. She accepts it, humbling as it is, knowing that she must learn beyond the superficial understanding she had the first time around.

Shortly after saying this, Tawanda's humility is tested during the director's afternoon class. He embarrasses her by saying she answers too quickly and she should think first: "You need practical knowledge. Keep it simple. Don't overcomplicate things." He is direct, and not unkind, but those in the room feel for her, knowing how his words sting.

The women are rehearsing a second song for the banquet, called "Future Generations." Sheila has a solo. Staffer Camila, Dennis's wife, has the solo for "Just a Prayer." Sheila has a lovely, childlike quality to her voice, perfect for this song's lyrics. Many women here have great voices. The ability to express in song what they cannot always say in words is healing.

A 5-minute van ride brings the women to the evening chapel service, which is informal, spirited. The director is also the pastor of this congregation. He requests prayer for victims everywhere.

The deacons and the director invite people to come to the front for individual prayer. It is a loud but pleasant time. Dennis (a deacon of the congregation) prays with one man and he falls back onto the floor in a dead faint. Later, some women say this is the first time they have seen someone "slain in the spirit." The prayers in tongues (glossinalia), are also a first for some, and they are eager to comment on it.

The women are told to pray with a partner. Rosa does not want to pray and asks me to pray with her. As I begin to pray with her I tear up. She says, "Why are you crying? Clean yourself up." I respond by asking if she ever cries. She says, "I cried so much in my past that now I don't have any tears left. Now I only cry when I'm angry." Then she laughs and says, "That's not funny." We both laugh.

I like Rosa. Even though she resists almost everything about the program, she is authentic. If she stays, she will do better than someone who scams the system by saying what people want to hear.

FIVE
IDENTITY

Thursday, September 27, 2001

The highlight of today is a field trip. The director and Dennis take us to see a life-size model of the tabernacle at the Mennonite Visitors' Center in Lancaster. En route, we drive within minutes of my house. It is a strange feeling not to be able to go home. I have a fleeting insight into how the other residents must feel that so much of the world representing health, wholeness, prosperity seems not just out of their reach, but foreign. On the other hand, they meet people or enter settings that serve as bridges, offering some hope of being able to transition into that world.

In the van, Brooke is reading Jacqueline Strothoff's booklet, "The End of a Nightmare, and the Beginning of a Dream." Jacqueline was a heroin and cocaine addict for fourteen years. She stole to feed her addiction and tells harrowing stories of a lover who died of an overdose as well as her own overdoses and attempted suicides. Hospital rehabilitation, community rehab, primal therapy, day treatment programs, residential 12-step programs, methadone treatment, and support groups didn't work. Yet she has been drug-free since she entered New Life for Girls in 1975 and encountered Jesus Christ. The most compelling part of Jacqueline's story is when she realized that her actions caused the death of her brother. She is healed of her addiction, but she also has come to terms with her guilt.

Brooke reflects, "I have an older sister and a younger brother. I thought about the fact that my actions could have affected them in that way. Now I plead with them not to drink and drive, not to follow my example. But they feel as if it's not going to happen to them."

On the bus ride to and from the Mennonite Visitors' Center, Rosa tells stories about caring for her uncle—she called him Tio—when he was dying of cancer. He was a Christian youth group leader. She postponed her college education to care for him. The family let that burden fall to her, and she resented this, but, at the same time, she had precious moments with her Tio. She recalls the last conversation they had together: "'You are afraid of death,' he accused me. He was right, but I denied it. 'Why be afraid of death?' He told me it is the one sure thing in our lives."

Someone asks Rosa about juggling college with working and caring for her daughter. She answers with a monologue, and intrigues her audience by the way she layers her thoughts to capture a nuance of feeling or meaning. It is as if she can't stop talking until she gets it exactly right.

"We live in a neighborhood now in what one time was good because it was all like, Jewish and Italian—wasn't really a lot of black or Puerto Rican then. Now you just cross the boulevard and boom, it's the ghetto. I saw my daughter every day. I came home almost every night. So to me it didn't really matter when I left on the weekends, because my mother and daughter have their own lifestyle. Even though we lived in the same house she had a whole different schedule because my mother was involved in the church and my mother was a teacher and my daughter was always with her. If I had evening classes I would go home, eat a little bit, and go to school. If I had a little time, I would go to the bar, then go home. Depending on where I woke up, I'd get up, do the morning thing, get ready, go to work, take a nap while I was going to work. I was so tired, always tired. I had to take two buses to get there by 8:30 a.m., and I'd be there until five o'clock. But instead of going straight home I would go to the bar. And drink and drink and drink and whatever, until they closed, or I had someone take me home, or I went home with someone.

And that was my routine every single day. It was the same thing over and over again.

"Every hour of my life had to be full so that I wouldn't think. Partying and work and going to school. I remember going to the bar and drinking and taking my finals. I was finishing my associate's degree; I was supposed to graduate last May, but I didn't even finish because by that time my drinking was... I just wanted to drink all the time."

She laughs and shakes her head. "Even on the campus, during the day, when I was supposed to do my homework, I'd sit at the computer lab for ten minutes, and I'd end up going drinking at a place on campus. They would give you a ticket to drink free.

"I only ate during work. I had to sit with the kids and eat with them and share with them. And my friend used to force me to drink some soup or something. My mom always had food ready on a plate, so all I had to do was warm it up in the microwave, but I would go straight to bed when I got home already messed up."

When the residents arrive at the visitors' center they spend a few minutes browsing the gift store before beginning the guided tour. The store has an impressive array of crafts, art and furnishings by artisans from all over the world. Moments later the guide ushers the group into an exhibit space. In it is a life-sized replica of the ancient tabernacle. The women take notes as she describes each item and its significance, because the director told them there will be questions about it on their next test.

Everyone enjoys the field trip. As they head back to the van, the director tells the residents that he came to faith in New York City through the witness of Mennonite missionaries, and that the Westminster church he pastors is modeled in that tradition. The bus is quiet on the ride back.

Once back, the afternoon parses out into bathroom time, singing practice, dinner, showers, study hall, and devotions.

Prior to study hall I chat with Brooke, Sheila, Tristes, and Tawanda. Brooke and Tawanda both observe, "You don't look like you use." I tell them I don't currently use, although there was a time when I experimented with alcohol. Tawanda adds, "I knew it wasn't alcohol or drugs, because you don't talk about your past."

Sheila remarks, "When I first saw you, you had a glow, peaceful ... everything seemed so organized."

Brooke asks why I am here. I tell her that I will be talking to the group on Saturday. I ask, "Do you need to know before then?" Brooke replies, "When the time is right, you'll know." Tawanda observes that I am "always writing" and wonders whether I am writing a book.

During study time, Kenda whispers that Lucille has been consistently late getting to meals, devotions, and study hall. Sometimes her excuse is that she is in the shower or she didn't know, or she has gas. People are getting tired of her loner behavior. That by itself might be easier to handle if she did not also have a manner that comes off as self-righteous. She questions the sincerity of others, and she prays in tongues loudly during the prayer sessions and lights out. Rosa finally told her to shut up. Her prayer is loud and confessional: "Thank you that I am not dead, that I do not have AIDS, that I had protected sex with my partners ... ." Now, during study hall, Lucille accuses Kenda of taking her pen. Later, when Lucille's pen turns up on her bed, Kenda unsuccessfully seeks an apology, voicing her resentment about the accusation. This kind of conflict could easily infest a group. The larger question in Lucille's case is whether she will be able to adapt. She has said repeatedly, "I hope I can stay in this program." She has also said she has trouble with the rules, that they are her biggest challenge.

The conflict between Kenda and Lucille escalates. It does not appear to have racial or cultural undercurrents (both women are African-American and are from urban Baltimore).

At snack time Lucille criticizes the testimony Kenda gave at the banquet rehearsal to staff and residents in the dining room. At first, she framed it by addressing the definition of testimony. "Why is it focused on the past?" But Lucille's philosophizing ends in criticism: "She did not give enough credit to God." Kenda overhears, walking into the dining room and telling Lucille she does not appreciate it. Staff member Maria asks them to drop it. Later, Kenda brings up the pen incident again, in Lucille's presence.

Just before bedtime, Maria leads devotions, reading Colossians 3:5–14. It is not lost on this audience that Paul wrote from prison. He encouraged members of the Colossian church to "put to death ... whatever belongs to your earthly nature: sexual immorality, impurity, lust, evil desires and greed, which is idolatry." He adds to the list anger, rage, malice, slander, and filthy language, observing that these traits belong to a past life, but that the follower of Christ has a new identity: " ... a new self, which is being renewed in knowledge in the image of its Creator. Here there is no Greek or Jew, circumcised or uncircumcised, barbarian, Scythian, slave or free, but Christ is all, and is in all."

Paul completes the identity metaphor with the plea to "clothe yourselves with compassion, kindness, humility, gentleness, and patience." Maria invites residents to share their thoughts. The comments bring to mind something Chere and the director said in class, that they have committed all of these wrongs multiple times. They are not bragging about past exploits, but about the power of God to change and heal. They were people that others thought were lost causes, treated like garbage. It is shocking to hear them describe themselves as garbage, to think of oneself as garbage: rotten, dead, disposed of. It is troubling to imagine navigating a life journey from that extreme. It puts into new perspective certain terms the group uses, such as "my mess" and "stink" and "wasted."

As on previous nights, the women form their thoughts around favorite passages of Scripture. Sheila mentions her special verse is Revelation 3:8, from the apocalyptic letter written by John during his exile on the island of Patmos. It describes God's prophecy: "I know your deeds. See, I have placed before you an open door that no one can shut. I know that you have little strength, yet you have kept my word and have not denied my name." Sheila sees her children as part of the promise of the open door and longs to be reunited with them. There is a legal barrier, although she doesn't go into detail in this meeting. The children are dispersed and in the care of different family members. The youngest has significant health problems.

Tristes cites Revelation 21:24–27 as her favorite, a description of the temple in the heavenly city, the New Jerusalem: "The nations will walk by its light and the kings of the earth will bring their splendor into it. On no day will its gates ever be shut, for there will be no night there. The glory and honor of the nations will be brought into it. Nothing impure will ever enter into it, nor will anyone who does anything shameful or deceitful, but only those whose names are written in the Lamb's book of life."

Tawanda reads one of hers, Chapter 14, from the book of Job, that famous sufferer. This is Hebrew poetry. The passage begins, "Man born of woman / is of few days and full of trouble." Life's irony is not lost on her. Through Job's words she articulates her own faith, weighted with questions born of despair and harsh experience: "Who can bring what is pure from the impure? / No one! So look away from him and let him alone, till he has put in his time like a hired man. ... if a man dies, will he live again? / All the days of my hard service / I will wait for my renewal to come."

Maria says that her favorite verse is James 1:19: "My dear brothers, take note of this: Everyone should be quick to listen, slow to speak, and slow to become angry." She appreciates the practical value of Scripture for guidance in everyday living.

Without elaboration, Rosa reads Psalm 4, verse 8, another selection of Hebrew poetry: "I will lie down and sleep in peace, for you alone, O Lord, make me dwell in safety." Then she reads another, Psalm 139, explaining that it was part of a prophecy spoken over her when she went to a charismatic pastor in Puerto Rico for healing and received the gift of tongues. She said that, even though the woman was praying for her in tongues, Rosa could understand what the woman was saying; her words were coming straight from Rosa's own heart. Some residents are familiar with this passage set to music, and can hear the music as she reads:

> *Where can I go from your Spirit?*
> *Where can I flee from your presence?*
> *If I go up to the heavens, you are there;*
> *If I make my bed in the depths, you are there.*
> *If I rise on the wings of the dawn,*
> *if I settle on the far side of the sea,*
> *even there your hand will guide me,*
> *your right hand will hold me fast ...*
> *For you created my inmost being;*
> *you knit me together in my mother's womb.*
> *I praise you because I am fearfully and wonderfully made.*
> —Psalm 139: 7–14

Rosa later admits to other residents that she is a Christian, but is concerned about her spirituality. She refers to Chapter 11 in Luke, a passage that suggests that demons can enter seven times stronger into a soul swept clean, then sullied.

Maria closes by focusing on the message of Colossians 3:14: "And over all these virtues, put on love, which binds them all together in perfect unity." She invites everyone to express compliments to each other and then prays for the group.

The consultant's voice in my head says this is a smart way to end the meeting, a call for appreciation and unity. My personal experience takes me back further, to an ordinary daily experience of my childhood, when my father would turn off the television and call the family together in the living room for family devotions: a Scripture reading and short message, discussion, and prayer. This was the time when we talked about the events of the day and made decisions as a family. Any friends visiting us at that hour became a part of the circle. As I grew older and experienced the world beyond my family, I discovered that this evening habit of family devotions was a rare occurrence. I would not encounter it again until now, in a treatment program for addicts, among women who had neither family nor community, and were recreating both.

SIX
OYSTER SKY

Friday, September 28, 2001

It is cooler today. The women are permitted to wear jeans as they set up for the banquet at Ascension Episcopal Church. An AA meeting is taking place upstairs while they work. There is a strong scent of tobacco (and, one woman comments, alcohol) on the folks who go upstairs. The church has a beautiful facility, spacious and well kept. Residents set up twenty-five tables with ten chairs to each. Holly and I are tasked with staple-gunning the pink plastic tablecloths to the tables. The staples will not even penetrate the table—they just fall to the floor. We laugh at the futility of our efforts. Next we are assigned to the balloon line where each table will have at its center a balloon bouquet, two pink and two wine-colored helium balloons tied with pink string. Tristes is "bossing" Rosa about how long to cut the ribbon. More laughter. The table favors look great; NLFG women made them in advance. They are scented candles in clay flowerpots with dried flowers arranged around the edge.

Choir practice goes reasonably well after decorations are complete. Nervousness over seeing family members runs as undercurrent for excitement about the event.

The sky is still overcast; it is an oyster sky, threatening rain. On the van ride back from the church Brooke wants to talk about her daughter, J. J., and what happened just prior to her coming to NLFG. Her monotone words tumble out like beads on a string.

"I was living by myself, living a so-called normal life. I was aggravated one day, because I asked my aunt to babysit and she threw a fit; I took the kids and drove off. I had money in my pocket, and a friend was helping me with finances so I wouldn't slip. Then I saw some guys I knew, gave them my money, and let them use my car to go buy drugs for me. Dumb thing to do." She fingers her necklace as she talks, shaking her head in disgust. I said, 'You guys can use my car. Just take me up to my house.' I had to work the next day. They told me a time they would come back. My mom called, knowing I was mad at my aunt. I lied about the car, said it broke down, ran out of gas. And it got later and later.

"I was using; once I start I don't want to stop. Might as well forget everything. Don't care about my kids, nothing. I just wanted to get high. And I didn't want to leave my house because it was night out: I was paranoid. My mom must have known something was up. I had some stuff on me, and I was spacing out. Pacing around the house. My mom and my sister came in the back way, and I had my pipe and stuff out. I met them in the basement. 'What are you doing here?' I got defensive. Then wouldn't you know, here come the people I gave my money to—two black guys, a white guy, and three Puerto Ricans. My mom saw they had my keys. I didn't care, I just wanted my drugs. My mom started yelling at me and she took my keys. Then Casey's dad comes by and he starts yelling, 'Crackhead!'

"Mom stayed until 2:00 a.m. or so. I pretended to sleep until she left. I used my last little bit, then I left my kids at home and went down the street. I was waiting for this other guy, but in the meantime, my daughter got up and walked to a bar. They called the cops. When they came to the house, it was a mess. I wasn't there. Child Services took the kids."

Brooke pauses, looking out the van window at the blur of lawn and houses flashing by. She sighs.

"After two days, I came back with this guy, a rich guy. He comes back to the house with me, but my kids are gone. Later my daughter told me, 'Mom, I was scared, but I'm glad Casey wasn't following me.'"

Brooke's eyes are pleading. "What kind of hurt have I put on that little girl, my kids? I was selfish. Didn't really care about anyone else's needs; I thought I was being a good mother when I was out there. Because I cleaned and cooked and did the laundry and went to work. So responsible. Maybe I could go a couple weeks without using, but then I would get the urge, and it would be hard for me to stop. When I didn't use, I was strict with my kids. They never knew what to expect. I was very selfish."

Someone asks what she was using at the time.

Brooke does not varnish the truth. "Alcohol and co-caine... and I used people; I didn't care. Just used them to get my drugs and money—whatever I needed that day. It didn't matter. The last couple months of my addiction is when I lost my kids. I lost my self respect, my dignity—everything. There would be days when I didn't sleep or eat. Drugs were on my mind: drugs, drugs, drugs. I had fears of cops, of picking up a cop. Am I going to get arrested? I never really stole—I would just get my money from men. It was easier to have sex than to steal." She closes her eyes for a moment. When she looks up again, regret veils her eyes.

"Four years of cocaine addiction. I used all hard drugs. Crack is cheaper, but cocaine was my thing. It's harder to get, costs more money. When they cook it up into crack you feed for it more, plus they're making more money.

"I started drinking and doing drugs after high school. When I was twenty-one I started going out to bars. Met J. J.'s dad, got pregnant at twenty-four. He left me when I was pregnant and I lived by myself for four years. I met a guy who was an addict—I didn't even know it. He told me he was an ex-addict, and I believed him. He would steal my money and get high." Her eyes widen. "I didn't know any of that was going on. Then we started using together. He got cocaine for other people. I always said no, but one night I tried it. That was it. Off to the races."

Someone asks, "He quit, then started using again?"

"Yes. One time he hit me in the face because he was so jealous. He hit me and I was everywhere. I called the cops, I could have put him in jail, but I didn't. A few days before Christmas he died of a drug overdose.

"My family, my aunt and uncle, used drugs. I would party a little at first, hated it. But with the powder, you just get hooked. It's so easy. Every few months, then every other weekend, then every week. Then I wanted it every day. And then I got involved with Casey's dad, and he used, too. We used together and drank.

"Cocaine is a social drug, but crack is not. You get what you get, and then you're bugged out—just high. You think the police are going to bang the door down any minute. Constant fear … "

She laces her fingers together, pausing on a new train of thought. "I'll be thirty next September. After I got pregnant with J. J. I didn't do drugs at all. Then one night I went out and smoked crack while I was pregnant with my son. I smoked all night. Casey's father said he was going to stop when the baby was born, and he did. I was the one who went on a crack spree."

"Is he still in the picture?" one woman ventures.

The van pulls into the parking lot. Brooke smoothes her jeans. "Yeah, he takes Casey every other weekend. He spoils him."

Preparing for the banquet is a major production and takes almost two hours. Everyone dresses up for the event in formal style dresses, high heels and necklaces. It's as if they are acting out their new identity. Certainly that is what makeup and formal attire can represent for women.

Kenda whistles when she sees me in the black sheath dress: "Wow, girl, you look like the wife of the President of the United States." I laugh and reply, "I'll take that as a compliment." Tristes pops her head into my room, sees my makeup bag, and frantically motions for me to come to the door. "Let me borrow your blusher. Please, Michele." I resist, remembering the rule about no borrowing. "Please Michele. I will just take a little right here." I allow her a fingerful of the blush cream, shaking my head. She knew just whom to ask: I am still on my first week of blackout probation.

That evening the banquet hall fills quickly. The residents have a table to themselves with Emily as chaperone; the rest of the staff sit nearby. They don't talk very much; instead they look around to see who arrives, and whether the arrivals have anything to do with the group.

Brooke and Holly sit with their families, beaming. Sheila and, as it turns out, Rosa—to her surprise—also have people there to see them. Mona shows up and greets everyone with a hug. Holly introduces her mother.

Worship begins and Brooke dances and sings with J. J., a miniature of her mom. Her younger sister and mother look subdued.

The banquet guests greet each song by the choir with loud applause, especially "Future Generations" and Sheila's solo. Every face in the choir seems to mirror the hope in Sheila's face as she sings. Next, Kenda steps forward. Her voice remains strong as she speaks her truth.

"My mother was a heroin addict. We weren't abused, we weren't neglected. She was always there, and she took care of us, but she was a heroin addict. She always made sure we had food, clothes, lights, and everything that we needed. She was always in her room with her friends. My brother and sisters were young; they didn't understand. I was eleven, and I didn't know what she was doing, but I knew not to knock on her door, because she was in there with her friends. All of the responsibility of caring for my brother and sisters was laid on me, but I did it because I love my family. We lived with my stepfather: He was there, but he wasn't. He never did anything, that bum. My mother and he fought all the time. And he abused me sexually. I did well in school, but, to mask my pain, I started experimenting with marijuana, then cocaine and heroin, pills—anything I could take—until I needed to support my habit with stealing and prostitution. I got a prison sentence of up to twenty years. My attorney—she must have been a Christian—advocated for me and got me into NLFG.

"Now," a smile steals across her face, she punches one fist in the air, "I'm a child of God, saved by grace! I'm a new creation! The old has passed away." She shouts over the applause, "Behold, all things have become new in my life!"

The fundraising goal for the banquet is $4900 to replace the boiler and mattresses. It nets a total of $4700. After the festivities, the women change clothing at the church to tear down and pack up.

On my way to the bathroom to change, a staff member stops me and says, "Are you ready? Tomorrow is your big day."

I say, "My heart is divided; I will leave part of it here."

She nods, "I know, that's why I stayed and have been working with New Life for eleven years." The director also says something to me: "Michele, this is so big, man. How are you going to do it?"

At bedtime I am thinking about how I have spent my adult life: overfull with work, too little reflection. As sleep settles over this house where habits die hard, I reckon with the poverty of my soul.

SEVEN
SECRET REVEALED

Saturday, September 29, 2001

*E*very activity today will have a bittersweet quality because it is the last full day here for me. I remind myself to pay attention. Emotional fullness has a tendency to pull me inward and avert my eyes to what is really going on.

The wakeup call is late since it is Saturday and because of the banquet the night before. After breakfast, Shantay, a part-time staffer, asks Sheila and Tawanda if they will help her move to an apartment offsite. They agree and soon all three are gone.

The other women clean the living room because the reception area is filled with donated items from last night. Reminiscing over the evening, the women are spirited.

"Write ups" and "disciplines" prompt some women (Kenda in particular, also Tawanda) to watch for the infractions of others—and report them. Kenda's discipline is loss of privileges and an extra month in the entry phase. She has a sweet spirit but a defensive wall so high others cannot get beyond it.

Kenda and some of the other single women—Sheila, Brooke, and Lucille—were eyeing the men at the banquet. This will be a logistical and cultural challenge for the new men's program. Few of the residents in the program are married but most have children with the exception of Mona, Tawanda, and Kenda.

Saturday is a fasting day, which means there is no lunch. After cleaning the women gather in the living room for devotions led by Daniella (with Dennis assisting). The devotions last an hour longer than scheduled.

I realize Dennis must have been biding his time until the director and other staff members arrive—the room and doorways are jammed with people now—because when the director shows and Brooke stops talking, Dennis turns to me.

Rosa agrees to translate for me. Now that it is my turn I become emotional and I explain that I cannot consider what God has done for me without emotion. (Which is true. But what is also true is that I am preparing to say goodbye.) I ask them, what is my addiction? They remember something I said early in the week, about my mountain being my self-esteem tied to work. I mention a book I read by an anthropologist, Claire Sterk, who observed women addicts. Sterk asks one addict the question, "Why do you keep going back to rehab, why can't you get clean?" The addict's response: "I am an addict, a mother and a wife in that order. To change, I would have to become a new person." Although the anthropologist did not comment on the statement, I sensed its significance, and suspected a connection to NLFG's mission and solution. Eventually, I approached the NLFG Directors about a research and writing project related to my doctoral program.

Rosa abruptly stops translating. The director picks up where she stops. I tell them that when I meet them again, at Dover, they will have the opportunity to grant me permission to interview them and be co-researchers with me. As I talk I notice that the women are all tearful; Rosa has begun to sob uncontrollably. "See, I can cry." I put my arm around her and try to comfort her.

The director turns his laser beam gaze on each of us as he speaks.

"I want you to know that the New Life for Girls leadership considered Michele's proposal very carefully, and prayerfully. We would not have allowed her here if we thought she would expose you or NLFG to risk in any way. It was my decision" he pauses for emphasis, "not to tell the residents and the rest of the staff about Michele's research purpose. I wanted her to be able to experience this place as any other resident experiences it. If what Michele writes gives credit to any individual or group of individuals" he fixes his gaze on me "it will be to her shame—because the program belongs to God, this is

God's work." He pauses again. "Does anyone have anything they want to say?"

Rosa speaks first. She looks down initially, her hands working as she speaks. She says, "When I understood what you were saying, I wanted to punch you. It brought to the surface all the past hurts and betrayals I have had in my life." Rosa looks at me (my arm still around her shoulders) "Then there were these different feelings that started to come out. I listened to you and began to see that what you are doing could benefit a lot of women. I began to see a picture of my own selfishness." She thumps her chest. "I began to experience healing."

Each woman has something to say about me, or about our relationship, that was affirming, and to indicate they understood and accepted my purpose. They all volunteer their stories for my use.

The director closes by saying that in my case, the women have permission to keep in touch with me through correspondence. And that they can take the rest of the day to be with me, ask questions, exchange hugs, say goodbye, bring closure. The mood of the room is sort of quiet joy—and the room is filled with love.

In fact, everyone does want to talk to me one-on-one. They take turns, but for the rest of the day I spend most of the time listening. It is a marathon of sorts (emotionally, intellectually, spiritually.) At times what they tell me is so difficult to hear that I can barely continue. For example, one woman tells me that her mother, as a single working parent, did not always have childcare available, and on those days she locked her in a closet "for safety."

The devotional time closes with the Bible passages about a woman who regarded herself as the world regarded her—as garbage, as a prostitute—but whom Jesus saw differently. As the resurrected Christ, he chose to reveal himself to her first. Another gospel account adds that when she told the rest of Jesus's followers, they did not believe her (Luke 24). But it did not matter. Before long, Jesus's story was circulating throughout the known world. So, too, the women of New Life share stories of what Christ has done.

The conversations continue over a dinner of shrimp and rice. Emily brings in a magazine with pictures of the September 11 terrorist attacks. For women who have been in the program since before that date, this is the first time they have seen any pictures of it.

Since Saturday is traditionally time for games and videos, after showers the residents congregate in the dining and living rooms. It is a good time to be able to lighten the pace with games and TV watching. Maria, her mother, Lucille, and Holly play spades. The rest play Chinese checkers. Then Rosa picks out a video, *Wild Hearts Can't Be Broken*. The women watch this until bedtime.

At bedtime, Tawanda, Sheila and I are saying goodbye and joking. Maria asks me to pray for the room. I do. The lights are out, and all is quiet in the house. But in the darkness I can hear the muffled sound of Tawanda and Sheila—crying themselves to sleep.

PART TWO

PHASE TWO: DOVER

"I weep for you," the Walrus said;
"I deeply sympathize."
With sobs and tears he sorted out
Those of the largest size,
Holding his pocket-handkerchief
Before his streaming eyes.

O Oysters, said the Carpenter,
"You've had a pleasant run!
Shall we be trotting home again?"
But answer came there none—
And this was scarcely odd, because
They'd eaten every one.

—Recited by Tweedledee in Chapter IV
of *Through the Looking Glass*

*If a man dies, will he live again? All the days of my hard service
I will wait for my renewal to come.*
—Job 14:14

EIGHT
NEW FRAMES

Sunday, December 30, 2001—Tuesday, January 1, 2002

*On Sunday, December 30, I am back at Westminster to wit-
ness four women I know receiving certificates for their successful
completion of the introduction phase (Rosa, Tawanda, Brooke, and
Holly. Kenda has already graduated to the main center at Dover),
and the women who are parents (Brooke, Holly) receive a certificate
for completing a parenting course.*

*After the ceremony I watch them rehearse a satirical skit about
life at the intro center which they have prepared for the next evening's
New Year's Eve party. The skit consists of three scenes: breakfast, study
hall, and devotions. The women really ham it up. It's funny. There are
basic underlying themes (e.g., the importance of obedience) but the
women say what they think, spoofing themselves and the staff. Later
Rosa comments: "We joke around about stuff like the food, but we
remember there were times when we were on the streets and didn't
have anything to eat."*

*I agree to be the person who takes them to the Dover Center on
New Year's Day.*

Alice's adventures in *Alice in Wonderland* and *Through the Looking-Glass* are reminders that when people look at the world
through the frame of a new experience, the way they see the
world changes—sometimes radically.

Those who graduate from the introduction centers such
as Westminster have a new appreciation for the life they have,
a heightened sense of purpose and potential, and a great sense
of accomplishment. They have mastered the first leg of the
recovery journey.

At 9:00 a.m. on New Year's Day, Rosa, Tawanda, Brooke, and Holly climb into a van to go from Westminster, Maryland, to Dover, Pennsylvania.

It's a clear-skied, sharply cold day. Holly's parents are already there waiting in their car, along with her 2-year-old son Bradley and her paternal grandmother. Today is an unstructured day for the Westminster residents. The only women awake are the ones going to Dover. They have the glazed look of tired excitement. As they load their luggage into the back of the van, there is a different mix of joy and anxiety in each woman. Tawanda, who had reached the junior staff level during a previous admission to the Dover program, is self-assured and full of advice. She is a den mother of sorts. Brooke is giddy with questions. Holly is eager with anticipation. Her parents, who will follow with Bradley in their own car, seem quiet and hopeful, cautious. Rosa appears anxious—she hasn't said a word all morning. Staff member Geena hands Michele, the driver, two bags, one with paperwork and one with medicines, instructing her to give them to whomever is in charge at Dover upon our arrival. The riders and their luggage fit snugly into the van. Each woman has two suitcases, several bags, and pillowcases filled with clothing. Holly rides shotgun. Tawanda, Rosa, and Brooke squeeze together an the middle bench. Tawanda offers to say a prayer for our trip. They're off.

The drive takes about two hours. There is cheerful chatter for the duration; at times the women break into song. They choose familiar songs so all can join in. Noticeable changes are evident in the women compared with earlier in the program. They have a vitality and confidence that was not there before. Tawanda speaks with a purposefulness that suggests she has been thinking about what she needs to say.

"Everything that you're thinking about Dover, throw it out the window, or leave it in this van, or whatever you have to do. It's not about how soon I will see my kids or my family. It's about growing close to God. Lily, the assistant director, is strict. She will not tolerate rule breaking. And I do not want to see you fail. If you are tempted to gossip or have any problem at all, go to your counselor. If you see other women doing something wrong, go to your counselor. Don't try to handle these things yourself. And if you see me doing something wrong, call me on it."

During Tawanda's talk I wonder what longer-term impact the dependence on counselors and each other would have on their eventual independence. I think about this again at the stop for gas, when the women ask me if they may visit the restroom. It is not clear whether this is habit from other supervised outings, or a courtesy to me as the driver, or whether they now perceive me as an authority figure. Time will tell.

Tawanda mentions health concerns and asks to be remembered in everyone's prayers. She will have laser surgery for cataracts in March and also some dental work done. To help correct an overactive thyroid, she is taking an iron supplement. "Pray I will stop losing weight," she asks. The thyroid problem relates to a caustic substance in her system that is also causing her teeth to rot. There is a free dental clinic NLFG residents are able to use once a year, she says. It sounds as if they will be pulling her teeth.

Paying for medical and dental work is always a challenge. Some of the women have insurance; NLFG also has a little, and some medical expenses are covered by pro bono work or donations.

They turn to the subject of gossip as a no-no in the program. Rosa mentions a time when she heard some gossip about a staff member and wanted to repeat it, but didn't. "I'm glad I didn't, because it turned out not to be true," she says. A few of the residents who left the program had difficulty with gossiping. Ironically, dealing with their departures was a breeding ground for gossip: whys, wheres, and hows. Was that malicious or unhealthy gossip? They wonder.

Of the women they mention who left the program, most did so to be reunited with their families. There seem to be certain policies or rules that keep some women from starting a program like NLFG, or keep others from staying in it. The women have definite opinions about this. Brooke insists that "Women leaving early to be with their children is not a policy problem. It's a lack of faith problem. They need to learn to trust that God can take care of them *and* their children."

Rosa agrees. "If we have trouble trusting God now, think how much more difficult it will be when we're on our own again." She adds a practical benefit: "Now we are learning how to be responsible parents. What if our children need us to be disciplined for their sake later on and we can't do it? They are being cared for now; why are we worrying about it?" Holly and Rosa both agree that it will be better for them to be reunited with their children later rather than sooner.

Rosa remarks, "Here's something God put on my heart." She describes a conversation with her counselor Dennis when she expressed extreme frustration with the program, with herself—with everything. "I told him I hate everything, and I went on and on about it. Finally he said, 'Rosa, what do you think God is calling you to do? What is your purpose?' I said I didn't know, but that lately I had been thinking about running a greenhouse. That's really funny, because I'm from the city, and I don't know anything about plants or running a greenhouse."

Tawanda echoes this theme of gaining a sense of purpose while in the program: "I like to cook, I'd love to run a restaurant. Before NLFG I didn't think about things like that."

Rosa, jumping to a new topic, exclaims that she is looking forward to being able to wear eyeliner at Dover. Tawanda laments that she had four new eyeliners that Dennis threw away right before she left. At Dover, we will wear eyeliner! Everyone laughs.

Rolling farmland gives way to dense woodland as the van snakes its way up and around the foothills where the Dover campus is located. Rosa expresses some trepidation about being in the woods. "It reminds me of the movie 'Jason.'" The other women squeal at that comment, then begin to fret about being all women in an isolated place. Brooke says, "Yeah, but when they hear about our prison records, they'll be scared." Their fear dissolves into giddy laughter.

The conversation turns to sexual purity. Rosa says, "One time I was in a car full of women from my mother's church, and I said I would have my daughter Zeta wear a chastity belt. Then my daughter, who was only ten or eleven at the time, embarrasses me by saying, 'I know what that is, Mom.' She's a teenager now, beginning to say and do some of the things I used to say and do. She tells people that I used to say I only wanted one child, a daughter, so that I could take her clubbing."

The others, too, express concern for the sexual purity of their children. Rosa recalls, "My mother told me I came from a guitar case and my brother from the hole in the guitar." She did not know what was happening when she began menstruating, yet she was already sexually active.

The van reaches the outskirts of Dover.

In other months the region looks lush and coolly green, but now the trees huddle in brown-gray ranks. It is easy to see why this austere landscape would intimidate city dwellers—any newcomer, really. A brick and concrete sign bearing the New Life for Girls logo appears on the right. The van takes the curving driveway past staff housing and a playground, and rolls up to the front of a 3-story dorm.

Carlos, a staff member, is in the parking lot to greet the women as they arrive, and jogs in ahead of them to the door to help with luggage. Holly's family members pull in to the next space. They have a look in their eyes that is often seen in the eyes of other addicts' relatives. It is an expression of guarded hopefulness, weary love. Their presence says I care, but their eyes convey a more complex story forged by years of disappointment and shattered trust. When family members show up at New Life, residents consider it nothing short of miraculous.

The women unpack the van quickly, filling the hallway with luggage. The group finds their way to the dining hall for something to eat. Since Dover had a New Year's Eve party, like Westminster, most residents (including Kenda) are still sleeping, but the women who are awake sit in the dining room and talk to the new arrivals. Holly's family leaves amid a flurry of hugs and goodbyes, while Tawanda reconnects with women who were once her students and are now staff.

Rosa offers words that define her: "After I had that conversation with Dennis, I felt conflicted, because I had criticized a program that has done so much for me. So I decided to apologize, which is hard for me. But the Holy Spirit was telling me to apologize to the director, not Dennis, because I had criticized the whole program. Also, because when I called to get into the program I was real with him, I wasn't wearing a mask; he's the only one I have been real with. The director accepted my apology. Then we started to talk about my hating everything. I told him, 'I don't know what to think or how to feel. This list of sins in the Bible, they describe me. How can I be different? How am I supposed to act?' I didn't want to fake it, but in order to be myself I thought I had to have a whole new identity. Then last Friday, Voni preached in chapel. She explained to me that God gave me my personality, that God will work through that personality. That helped a lot."

Rosa and I carry our trays to the kitchen and say our goodbyes. As I leave, Tawanda breezes up to me. "Hey, Michele, do you have fifty cents you could give me to buy a soda? I don't have a cent."

I hesitate, remember that this was against the rules in Westminster and probably is here, and tell her no. I remind her that we are co-residents and co-researchers, and we need to follow the rules. I teasingly add, "Besides, my week of probation ended a long time ago."

"Okay, that's cool." She smiles her goodbye. It appears that everyone is making a smooth transition, although Rosa still seems a little anxious. As it turns out, I have reason for concern.

NINE
BACK DOWN THE RABBIT HOLE

Wednesday, April 10, 2002

I arrive at the Dover center at 10:00 a.m. and meet my roommates, Shasta and Jessie. Jessie helps me move my things into our room in Joy hall, the staff hallway. She tells me a bit about the Dover center, such as its relative size: The population here is more than four times the size of introduction centers such as Westminster.

Shasta and Jessie are two of the staff members at Dover. Jessie is in her late thirties with fair skin, her dark hair in a pixie haircut. She is from New England originally and has a son who is a college freshman. Jessie came to New Life through a Teen Challenge introduction program and has been there for two years (including residency). She said it was hard to leave the Teen Challenge center, a beautiful Victorian house in a setting familiar to her, to come to Dover. At first she hated it: She came at a time when there was no hot water for showers because of a water shortage problem. To her surprise, she remained at New Life and now enjoys her staff counseling and teaching roles: "It's what I always wanted to do—just came to it a different way. God's way."

Jessie would like to start an introduction program in Massachusetts. "There's nothing in the state like NLFG for women that I know of," she says. Worcester is an especially needy area, with a lot of substance abuse. Her husband lives in a different state with their son.

When she returns to New England one of Jessie's dreams is bringing street people to church. She is prepared for the possibility that she may have to confront the church's reaction: "You know, they will come as they are from the streets, scantily clad, whatever."

Shasta is from California and is a contrast to Jessie: much quieter, she has honey-brown, shoulder-length hair and is athletically built. Shasta has just made the decision to go to the New Life center in the Bronx, New York.

Chapel takes place in a large meeting room on the main floor of the dormitory. The front wall is natural stone, with contrasting yellow sandstone and gray limestone forming a cross. Opal, the keyboardist, has a jazz-like improvisational style. She took lessons for eight years and is learning to play by ear. The U.S. and Christian flags flank a raised platform. A podium occupies the center; ceramic sculptures of angels and praying hands sit atop the organ. The whir of oscillating wall-mounted fans reveal that the space is not air-conditioned.

Just as at Westminster, the women who speak look straight ahead and not into the audience, even when audience members engage them. As at Westminster, they attach very little emotion to their personal stories. They show more emotion when talking about what God has done for them. Rosa is one of the women who speaks during sharing time. She knows she has trouble receiving love and believing that others will find her lovable. She describes a recent spiritual breakthrough: realizing that God loves her *even if* nobody else does.

The central speaker is Joseph, one of the few male gradu-ates of NLFG, who says he was a "120-pound bruise" when he arrived. Healed and no longer emaciated, he's reached a healthy 160 pounds.

Joseph is grateful. Citing Scripture, he tells the women to be strong and cultivate inner endurance. Overcome the past. Love yourself. It's a command: Love God with *all* your heart—"and *never,* " he raises his voice and hand, pausing for emphasis, "*never* forget where you came from!

"Sometimes we think we're all that and a bag of chips. Then the devil comes along and eats our chips! The only power the devil has is what we give him. Go through the mountain or climb over!" He thunders, "Kill the desire to get high, seek God's deliverance, and looking back at hard times, you can say, 'It's my turn to take back from the devil.' Remember the benefits of serving Christ."

Shouting and applause greet the director when he reports that he received medical test results back and he does not have cancer. Then he announces that Marcia, a staff member, is leaving New Life to go into full time ministry as an evangelist. Her parting words stay with the group, "God is some kind of wonderful."

The director looks at me and smiles. Previously, Lily, the assistant director, had explained my research plans to residents. The director calls me to the podium and invites me to introduce myself.

Lily advised me that my education may be intimidating to some, so I use humor to defuse the issue: "I didn't bring issues to a New Life service, how dumb is that?"

I touch on these points: that they are co-researchers with me; that they will see me with my work tools (notepad, tape recorder, consent forms); that their participation is voluntary; that not much research has been done on faith-based residential treatment programs and none on programs for women; and that this study will inform theory about "community" formation in organizations.

Tawanda, Holly, and Brooke have now been at Dover for four months and are all doing well. Rosa left Dover in January, just a few weeks after she arrived. She left abruptly and dropped out of sight. The residents felt a deep sense of sadness and loss knowing they may never see her again. The directors and staff seemed saddened, too, but they had experienced this many times before. Entrusting residents to God's care is second nature to them.

So they were not surprised when Rosa returned.

"It was tough," Rosa reports. "Going back through West-minster, then coming back here on Easter Sunday. I know my daughter prays for me. I want to do well here, for her. She's doing better in school. It was tough for her, too. Her grandfather was put into a nursing home. He died, and my daughter was never allowed to visit him." She explains that some family members do not recognize her daughter as a legitimate family member because she was born out of wedlock.

Rosa is now in the Alpha, or beginning, phase at Dover, while her peers from her first Westminster admission have progressed to Omega, the middle phase. This means they will graduate in October, but she will have to wait until next April. The phase after Omega, called Emmanuel, represents the time when residents decide what direction their lives after New Life will take. During the final residency phase, Reentry and Observation (R&O), residents serve as junior staff.

No lunch. Wednesday is a big breakfast, skip lunch, fast day. In the afternoon the women go outside for chores. There are signs of spring's new growth, its unfolding beauty. A red maple leafs out against a deep blue sky. Residents must clear out debris along the exterior of a dilapidated shed and wheel the full garbage can to the incinerator. Then they go back and rake the leaves into a big pile. Quiet Shasta helps. She is in her late twenties. She tosses her cascading honey-brown hair, the same color as her eyes. Her face is attractive though resolute; her rare smile seems guarded. She claims to keep to herself because she feels she is still a baby spiritually. She does not have any children. Shasta is intensely private. Is it shyness, politeness, or anger? A combination of the three? She works hard, raking vigorously.

The women finish earlier than planned and take their muddy shoes off at the back door. Beyond the Joy hallway's swinging double-doors are the cafeteria, the library, an office, and two staircases leading to the upper level, which houses residents' hallways, administrative offices, and the chapel. Like Alice's rabbit hole, the stairs are befuddling—both lead to essentially the same part of the second floor, which contains offices and resident rooms.

In contrast to the hallways, the cafeteria is a bright and noisy space. It's inviting, though somewhat overwhelming, especially to newcomers. Residents may sit anywhere. There are cozy booths along the wall or larger round tables dotting the center of the room. The booths have a deja-vu familiarity because they were donated by a McDonald's restaurant undergoing renovation. A group, including Tawanda, sits at one of the round tables enjoying a dinner of turkey, stuffing, and potatoes. Tawanda says things are going well for her (although she had a discipline today and had to write verses relating to disobedience.) "You know we had class this morning, Omega group did. Carlos taught the class." She talks about her tenuous financial position, saying she is in debt $11.00. Her "spiritual mother," the director of the Chicago introduction center, sometimes sends her money.

After dinner I volunteer to wash dishes with Sue. She is amiable, flaxen-haired, and also the mother of sons. She dries, I put them away. I am rooming in the junior staff hall, yet volunteering for chores is not something a junior staff person would ordinarily do. In fact, I am neither staff nor resident. No one seems confused or bothered by the ambiguity. I think this is aided by the fact that staff and residents abide by the same rules. If I cause a rule infraction, both residents and staff notice and correct me.

A few of the women walk around the campus after dinner. A pickup game gets underway on the basketball court. Africa, a junior staffer who will graduate in April, describes being in another Christian program. "It's the only one in Philadelphia for women," she says. "It does not compare with New

Life because it's too easy—there are no work assignments, no classes, and a much looser accountability."

Jade and Elsa are two other junior staff members completing their residency. They arrange plastic chairs on the concrete slab just outside the Joy Hall doorway and watch the sun set through the trees. From here they can also see the basketball court and, beyond the trees, the playground. When the last light fades, everyone becomes chilled and goes inside, settling in the lounge. The lounge is a simple, square room with a couch, table, and three chairs. These are bordered by a microwave and refrigerator. A low wall bisects the space, creating a small washup area with three sinks. Across the hallway, the lavatory includes three more sinks, three showers, and three toilet stalls, serving a hallway where twelve people live.

Jade talks about surviving five different prisons and a number of mental health and rehabilitation institutions. She has a languid voice with a slight lisp, and she apologizes for "not having her teeth in." Jade half-closes her eyes, catlike, when trying to remember something. She mentions shyly that in prison her appearance—not her singing—earned comparisons to Whitney Houston. She recalls a former persona. "My name was in the papers a lot. I'm not proud of it. I was the 'Mustang Bandit.' The police had trouble catching me and my boyfriend. See, we robbed these different locations, and we were always in our black Mustang. I served a total of eight years. I wants to get back to minister to women prisoners. Their self-esteem is stripped away. That happens in all the prisons, the same pattern."

Jade admits that when she had insurance she often pretended to have psychosis to get into better rehabilitation programs. She shows her family pictures, including one of her daughter "who could still go to Brown, but she got pregnant in high school. She's a talented writer." Jade herself loves to write: "Expressing my feelings is easier for me in writing than out loud. And like I say, a lot was published *about* me I'm not proud of. Hey, want to see my certificates?" She shares her prison and college IDs, her notebook full of certificates for courses completed during prison.

Fifty-something Elsa, bubbling with an enthusiasm belying her age, says this is her second time at NLFG, with a dozen years in between. Comparing her first and current experiences, she observes that "the program is exactly the same. I think it shows women reality, and that's why it is effective." Her husband, a former heroin addict, went through Teen Challenge. After their graduations, they started a ministry, but that was too much too soon, she says. They recently got divorced. They would relapse at alternating times. Then her mother died of cancer. In a small voice she says, "I wanted to die then." She lived out of her car for a while and was estranged from her children. "I decided to go back to NLFG after I got a confirming call from my daughter."

Jade interjects: "I decided to enter NLFG because I was so tired."

When the residents go back outside for a voluntary devotional circle, they stand, holding hands. The women are "striped," that is to say, they do not segregate themselves into ethnically defined groups. Children run in the center of the circle during songs. They laugh when Annabelle requests the "Hail Mary" song (she means a song called "Hail Jesus").

Assistant director Lily stops by on her way in from her evening college class. She greets everyone warmly. She goes to the kitchen to pluck some grapes from a new delivery of fruit. They are overripe, and she has to pick through them to find those worth eating. As she unwinds, Lily talks about her desire to have a sensitive heart, to be able to receive love and give love to God and others. Sensitivity is highly prized in this culture, because emotions were deadened in their lives as addicts. What a contrast to the world of business and industry, where people have been conditioned to devalue and hide their sensitivity, as if it is something shameful.

Everything is clean and orderly here. Or, as Lily observes, it is a sanctuary. She finds a perch on a stack of milk crates in the walk-in cooler. "When people come they say, 'It's different here.' God does that. It's like a shining city on a hill." She is specifically referencing the Phoenix location where she recently served as director, but says it applies to all of the centers. "New Life is both community and family," she says.

I climb into my upper bunk, above Shasta and jot down some field notes. The junior staff hall where I stay is called Joy; the two residents' halls upstairs are Love and Kindness, and the administrative hall is called Faith. The building is cross-shaped, with the chapel occupying the center axis of the upper story. I sketch the layouts of the hallways and our room.

I fall asleep wondering, is this more of a community or a family? Or a cult? And thinking about how identity change is so entwined with being here.

TEN
SANDPAPER SISTERS

Thursday, April 11, 2002

G lad I brought my earplugs. Footfall begins at 4:00 am. Continues through the early morning, the residents' time for showers and morning jobs (e.g. breakfast, relief of the night watch staff).

Our room has a high bureau, a low bureau, bunk beds where
Shasta and I sleep. Closet has a valance curtain—no closet doors at
NLFG. Jessie's bed forms a circle of furnishings that include a chair
and TV above a dresser, two smaller bureaus. I get in and out of the
bed with difficulty, so during the night I carry the chair over, and
that's where my toilet paper sits now. (As at Westminster you must
bring your own TP. I kept forgetting yesterday. First time—had to use
a page from my notebook!)

It is 7:30 a.m. Elsa is in the lounge giving her brunette bangs
a flick with a curling iron. Inez comes in to say that Marilyn's "Cults and Errors" class is starting. The class involves the
eight women in Omega phase. There are several subphases in
Omega and R&O. The number of months in R&O depends
on whether the resident intends to pursue school, work, or
a full-time staff position at NLFG. The levels are Alpha I–III
(one level per month, three months total); Omega I–III (one
level per month, three months total); Emmanuel; and R&O
I-VI (one level per month, six months total).

New Life draws the name for its groups from their bibli-
cal contexts: Emmanuel means "God is with us" in Hebrew;
Alpha and Omega mean the first and last, respectively, in
Greek. All are symbolic names for Jesus Christ.

Marilyn's class meets in the library, a plain room with two

large tables pushed together so that as many as a dozen students can sit in a U-shape around it. Against this bland backdrop, Marilyn gleams. With burnished brown hair and glowing caramel skin, she looks trim and professorial in a tailored suit. She stands at the head of two large tables, a blackboard behind her. Opposite her is a wall lined with thumbworn books, divided by topic on the shelves. All titles appear to have a spiritual emphasis.

Speaking in a soft, measured voice, Marilyn begins by reading a selection about freemasonry. The freemasons began as a guild of cathedral builders, intent to keep work through membership. A secretive, all-male organization, it evolved into a business guild with a charitable bent, founding Masonic hospitals and schools. Marilyn describes some of its cultlike aspects: a leader known as Worshipful Master; initiation involving a noose, spear, and threats. Although freemasonry represents its origins as Christian, Marilyn notes that Jesus is not the only savior in the freemasons' belief system. They believe good works earn an individual's salvation.

A class taught by Jessie, "Relationships," meets in the chapel from 9:00 to 11:00 a.m. There are twelve students in this Alpha class, including Rosa. They sit lined up behind each other, two or three in a pew, forming ragged columns, and maintaining a certain distance.

Lithe and animated, Jessie bounces around the room, gesturing as she talks. "Healthy and unhealthy friendships. Co-dependence. That's a biggie for us. You're looking to a person for something only God can give you." She tells the class that she used to have problems with jealousy: "Pray about your sister rather than gossiping." Discernment, she adds, is different from judgment.

In pairs, the women go through the "I am" list (a list of affirming qualities in a document titled "Who I am in Christ") to build each other up. "You are two friends building up self-esteem," Jessie encourages. She describes the deepest level of relationships as intimate friendship and fellowship, citing Galatians: "carry each other's burdens" (Gal 6:1, 2).

Jessie's animation and enthusiasm grow with each point she makes. "I woke up with a great sense of excitement this morning. You know how great that is? With drugs we were anesthetized to our feelings. Sometimes we're feeling for the first time and the emotions are intense. Ephesians 4:13–15 tells us that rather than being tossed around, as by waves, we must instead speak the truth in love. Proverbs 27:5–6 reminds us that a friend has your best intentions at heart: Wounds from a friend can be trusted, but an enemy multiplies kisses."

A few students can hear Iris snoring behind them.

Jessie refuses to answer a question that is about a counseling relationship, chiding, "That's not appropriate for this class. I won't go there." This does not sound harsh but does evidence boundaries. She talks about masks we wear and false personalities: "Gushers: you know the type, very affectionate. This is also someone who blurts out phrases without sensitivity. Then there's the Pressurizer: She gives to get."

One woman, Annabelle, points to a classmate and says, "That's you." Something fascinating begins to happen—these classmates begin unmasking each other! Over the murmur, Jessie continues: "We all wear masks. Take the Ramrod, for example. She is given to extremes. Any extreme is not good. I tend to be compulsive with exercise. You see? I just switched addictions. Anything or anyone can be an idol."

Jessie's vocal intonations are amusing, and dramatically comic. To her audience's amusement, she darts from row to row, imitating the mask she is describing. "Why do we wear masks? Because the world admires cool. James Bond. Then there are the fears of rejection, or repelling. We need to become transparent. We were like actresses out there, right?"

Patti, a student, mutters, "In here, too." Jessie does not hear her. She continues, "Lonely people live shorter lives."

Jessie lists for the class five ways to deepen relationships:

1. Give top priority to relationships.
   ("Love is always worth it.")
2. Dare to talk about affection.
3. Learn the gestures of love.
4. Create space in your relationships.
   ("The tendency to control ruins.")
5. "Cultivate transparency" (James 5:16) and confess to one another. ("Honesty is a gateway to healing.")

At this point, Jessie makes an assignment: Sit with someone you don't ordinarily sit with, get to know them a bit, and write your observations. A groan of protests rises up from the group. Roughly half of the class insists, "We're not ready." Jessie remains unfazed. "It can be anyone in boot camp except staff." (Jessie is the only person who uses the term boot camp to describe NLFG. She explains, "I don't like the word 'program.'") In spite of resistance and lots of questions, including a discussion about cliques at New Life, the assignment stands and the class is dismissed.

The women return to their rooms to prepare for chapel.

A tense scene begins to unfold in a room on Love Hall. A resident, Jonelle, is shouting, objecting to doing her jobs. Her counselor, Paula, stands outside her doorway, attempting to reason with her. Suddenly Jonelle appears at the door, her dreadlocks swinging. She lunges at Paula and takes a swing at her. Paula jumps back and avoids the blow. They stare at each other for a long moment. Paula put her hands up, says nothing, and strides away, her ponytail bouncing. Word of the incident travels quickly among the residents. Most residents express admiration for Paula: "She kept her cool and walked away."

Jade is sitting on the sofa in the lounge. As she talks to residents from Jessie's class about the unmasking, and about

Jonelle's outburst, she smiles knowingly and says, "We call that being a 'sandpaper sister.'" It is someone who rubs you the wrong way at first but is able to sand the rough edges in a spirit of caring. She adds, "Everybody here has at least one sandpaper sister."

Jessie enters in a rush, saying that her counselee Jonelle says she is leaving, and that her other counselee, Iris, may also leave. Jade observes: "People are different, like, in terms of their readiness to change. Some women just want a rest, want to stop—that was my reason. But drugs are not the only problem." She picks up a jar with a shaker top. "Let's say the woman is this jar. A secular treatment program can shake the cocaine out of the jar"—she shakes it vigorously—"but saying you're cocaine-free is not the same as having the underlying problem solved. It's almost a survival skill, drug use. To deal with the madness of life. The inside job is hard, sometimes you don't want to deal with the work. After you shake out the cocaine, what fills the void? Jesus does. We're not just here for ourselves, but to be a blessing to others. Drugs is just another mask." She segues from the general to the specific, talking about her family. She says that many of them are officials in the judicial system, several are councilmen." They are "hoity," by which she means high society or snooty. The implication is that she saw herself differently, not measuring up to their standards.

All residents are expected to attend chapel, barring illness or absences such as a choir trips. Today, thirty-eight women attend. The number is continually changing, as new women arrive and others leave for work or school, travel with the choir, or drop out. The headcount does not include the children or staff.

During the worship portion of the service, a tambourine is handed to me. This is the first time in my life I have ever used an instrument in a church service. Instantly, it changes the way I worship, as I become aware of wanting to stay in rhythm, but also aware of my role in the group. As I get more comfortable with the instrument I experience the group dynamic of worship in a new way. I am no longer alone with my thoughts, but aware of group thought as conscious expression. If the worship were not God-focused, this would be just another form of distraction; or in the extreme, group-think. Instead we are able to worship as a whole group and also as distinct voices with distinct contributions. It fascinates me.

At lunch a resident named Winona describes herself as a "city girl," from outside New York City. She does not like the city, associating it with confusion and drugs. Her sons, fourteen and four, are here with her. Fourteen-year-old Eric is the oldest male child to ever stay at the Dover Center. "At first they said no. So I just prayed about it," Winona says. Her story illustrates flexibility in the system.

Brooke is still not feeling well. She has plateaued—something is holding her back from complete healing. "I am praying it through, I haven't talked to my counselor about it yet."

Kenda is fuming: "I got an F on a paper. First F I ever received in my life!" Kenda's counselor wants to know why she didn't come to her. Kenda shoves her tray in frustration. "I thought I could handle it myself."

Africa, another lunchmate, was homeless until a pastor in Philadelphia gave her shelter. He got her into another faith-based program that serves as an introduction center for NLFG. The network of faith-based treatment programs may be "under the radar" of so-called secular programs, but faith-based programs are very aware of each other and seem to collaborate, as far as referrals, idea-sharing, pulpit exchanges, and so on. Africa says it's important to have "street knowledge" to counsel effectively: "I was in a lot of secular programs with counselors who did not have street experience. I knew they couldn't help me." Respect and willingness to change are the keys to effective treatment in her opinion, and NLFG's approach exemplifies this.

In the few minutes prior to work period, some residents venture out to enjoy the unseasonably hot, sunny day. The glider swing fills. Gisetta mentions that she was offered drugs at a secular outpatient "behavior modification" program. Many of the women talk about the problem of drugs being accessible in treatment programs, both secular and faith-based. Drugs are not available here. Visitors are screened and monitored, and prescription medications are kept in a locked closet and administered by staff. Gisetta stayed drug-free for four years, then relapsed. She dismisses methadone and other such treatment therapies. "Treating a drug problem with drugs makes no sense!" she exclaims.

After completing nursery duty and other jobs, a small group of women go shopping at the West Manchester Mall. Only women in good standing may go. The seven who go are a microcosm of NLFG: diverse in age, ethnicity, and socioeconomic background. Shopping is a culture journey in itself. Residents only go into stores that fit a certain price point (Payless Shoes, Dollar Store, Wal-Mart), but it's the store called Shoe Depot that garners raves. Throughout the trip Anabelle picks at Kenda, teasing her about her attitude. Kenda is still aloof, a loner, but earlier today she described herself as having matured. Anabelle's teasing is another dimension of the "sandpaper sister," a woman whose comments get under your skin but whose intentions are to encourage and spiritually refine you. Kenda and Anabelle pair off for the most part.

Spirits are high during the return ride. Tawanda bought a clothesline for double-dutch jump rope. Marcia wisecracks about the risks of jumping rope ("Uh-uh, I will not come to your aid. Maybe I will shove a bandage under your door, and that is it!") Marcia tells everyone to look for the house with the pet pig on the porch. After they spot the pig, Chicago-born Tawanda asks if a sow is a cow. The others tell her this would create a whole new breed of animal, and imagine the possibilities—Tawanda's sow cow farm. As they joke and tease, a beautiful sunset lights the way home. Indeed, the center is the place many residents call home, whether it is their home-away-from-home, or the only place that ever felt like home.

After the outing Ruth, Deirdre, and staff member Denise sit in the dining room, talking about Denise's garden. She and Marilyn live in a mobile home on one side of the main building. Lily lives in the small house next door, and Carlos and his wife Teresa live in a small house on the opposite side of the main building. Denise claimed a patch of earth between the dorm and her house to start a vegetable garden. She tilled the earth by hand and also built and installed a chicken wire fence to keep the deer and rabbits at bay. She is modest about her accomplishment: "I'm just a country girl from Virginia," she drawls. She looks like a wrangler without a horse in her denim jacket, jeans, and shoulder-length gray-blonde hair.

Later in the week Denise mentions that she was an alcoholic, addicted "for as long as I can remember ... I would just sit on the sofa, watch TV, and use." She marvels at the responsibilities she has had as a full-time NLFG staff member: "Counseling? Gardening? Teaching?" She chuckles, scratching her chin. "Back then, I didn't have a single thought in my head!"

It occurs to me that most of these ladies are probably keener people-observers than I am. In order to survive they had to be able to "work" (manipulate) people, and the "system"—welfare, legal, whatever systems they found themselves in. I wonder whether treatment counselors are more easily fooled if they lack a substance abuse past. (When I ask one of the directors, she reminds me that of the original staff, only the founding directors had a substance abuse past. However, she did acknowledge that consulting psychologists sometimes complicate their work because counselees have fooled them or played them against their New Life counselors.) I wonder whether any of them will attempt to "play" me.

Frequently I hear a recurring comment from women here—the residents, mostly: "I really admire what you're doing." They mean the research, but also that I'm staying with them. Acceptance is a process. I am often alone in the lounge, alone in the cafeteria, on a different schedule from most others. Right now it's 10:15 p.m. The smoke alarm chirps so incessantly that everyone becomes used to it. I hear voices talking behind closed doors, socializing. The smell of popcorn permeates the air. If I get invited to a room, that will mean something.

During the night I have a dream. It springs vividly to my mind when I awaken. In my dream, I keep gazing at a huge bowl filled to the brim with colorful polished but uncut gemstones—diamonds, emeralds, rubies, sapphires. I marvel at their beauty and value. As I admire them, I become aware that the gemstones represent the women of New Life for Girls.

ELEVEN
GEMSTONES

Friday, April 28, 2002

I get up at 7:00 a.m. and go to the lounge. Inez is ironing. Etta is doing her hair, Etta's daughter is eating cereal. Africa comes in to describe a situation with a difficult resident (Jonelle, the woman who took a swing at Paula). All in the room are women of color except me. What's interesting is that I am less aware of race (my own, others) than when I first arrived. Instead of noticing this detail as I enter the room, it occurs to me much later, an afterthought.

Africa reports that Jonelle "overslept, missed her job; at first someone said, let her be. But we said, no, as long as she's here she should do her responsibilities. Then we got a call from the director, who said, there's a bus at 5:00 a.m. and she's getting on it. So that's what happened."

"That's right" Inez says, "You got to do the program. Lord be with her."

"Yes." says Etta. "That's all that can help her now."

Carlos's "Leadership" class (the Omega group) meets in the library. He explains why memorizing Bible verses is important: They come to mind as needed for healing, fighting temptation, and so on. The assignment for next class is to pick a leader from the Bible and describe what leadership qualities he or she embodies. How did God shape the person? How would you pattern your life after him or her?

Carlos relaxes his tall frame against the blackboard. He has a winsome smile and a gentle yet direct approach to teaching. He details the theme of the assignment carefully: "The same faithfulness God used with this leader he will use with you. Your first year serving the Lord is your most crucial year. If you don't have a good prayer life, if you don't communicate your faith, you never will. You'll think that sharing your faith is an extracurricular activity, not a way of life. You can tell yourself, 'I am not going to be a hypocrite. I can walk in full obedience.' These are all leadership qualities. Stability: You can't lead anyone if they can't trust you. Consistency: When I see someone like that I can trust God more. You'll be saying, 'If God can keep him stable then he can keep me stable. I don't have to worry about being a hypocrite.'"

Carlos chooses to focus on stability for this class period. "Stability is resistance to sudden change, consistency of character. Steadfastness, reliability, dependability. When we are stable, we face our problems. If women fall after the program it's generally not through drugs, but through a pattern where your addiction can attack you again, such as eating disorders or men," he says. "Our identity in Christ does not change. If you have peace today you can have peace tomorrow, in spite of storms in your life. Manage your emotions. Ask yourself, does it line up with the character of Christ and the Word? Trust in the Lord. Spend time with God. He will give you confidence, and you will know his voice."

Carlos challenges the group. "Instead of running away from our fears, how do we overcome?"

Brooke tells the class she recently had a spiritual breakthrough, a release from fear. Carlos provides the analogy of casting your net into the deep and pulling up fish, or searching for gold nuggets: "God will not give you more than you can handle. If you find a nugget, it makes you want more. Maybe you beat drug addiction, God says that wasn't your problem. Dig deeper."

The women read from 1 Timothy about the requirements for becoming a leader. Carlos expounds: "We are being prepared for leadership in this program. Through classes, studying, consistency with work. To be a good leader, you need to know that everybody has the capacity to be one. In the body of Christ there are different parts. Gifts are different for each of us. Be a servant, be teachable, receive correction. Sometimes we say, 'I know' in defense of our actions. If you know, then why are you doing it?"

The group discusses examples of servant leaders from their own experiences. Gisetta describes a humble leader in government who was her employer. Carlos gives the example of being asked to be an assistant manager, even though others had seniority. "They gave the job to Jesus. He's the one with the leadership abilities, do you know what I am saying? They gave me the keys to a 5-million-dollar store. Didn't they check my past?" The class laughs, appreciating that a strong faith and work ethic can speak louder than police and credit records.

Carlos addresses wrong motives: "The leader is not one who manipulates; spiritually, manipulation is a form of witchcraft. We know how to manipulate, don't we? We knew what to say to police. We rehearsed it in the mirror!" As the class laughs, Carlos goodnaturedly grunts, "Busted! Or it's like this: 'I'm only going to smoke one rock'"—he spreads his arms wide—"'THIS big!' Years later we're still smoking rock! Jesus gives us tests so we can see his power."

After class, Carlos tells me that leadership is a new teaching topic for him, and he sees how challenges in his personal life have prepared him to teach. He asks, "Are you getting what you need for your work?" I tell him I am.

I am mulling over the implications of a hypothesis of mine, that these women represent the unconscious side of society. And, since all parts of a system are interrelated, they represent the unspoken, unconscious, parts of us.

In the spiritual sense, how is allowing drugs to control our lives all that different from allowing academics or work to do so? In the emotional and intellectual sense, how is allowing drugs to deaden our minds and emotions all that different from allowing cynicism or intellectual snobbery or the nightly news to numb our feelings and thinking? What about materialism? The predominant society is hooked on spending and consuming. In the extreme, materialism isolates and objectifies people.

The physical, social, and emotional consequences of substance abuse may be more obvious, but these other, more "socially acceptable" forms of addiction and social dysfunction cost our society a great deal, too. What separates the "functioning" person from the "addicted" may just be the success with which they color inside the lines and go unnoticed. The community-building framework that emerges from New Life is more than just an exercise in teaching former addicts to color inside the lines.

The speaker for chapel turns out to be Carlos, filling in for someone. His remarks, based on Luke 5, extend ideas from the leadership class: "Just as in preparation of the fishing nets, Jesus washes us, stretches us, then throws us out and uses us again. Preparation: That's a frustrating phase, isn't it? Even dope fiends have commitment to what they are doing. Go deep—drop your nets to the bottom, overcome fear."

Carlos speaks with intensity, his dark eyes blazing. "It's not about addiction," he says. "It's about sin. Drugs weren't the problem. Don't stop at just getting the anger out. Get the lust out. Get the greed out. We got too comfortable in shallow waters because we knew we could swim to shore. God's looking for someone obedient, and there's no compromise. It will cost you something."

At lunch Rosa explains how God saved her life. When September 11 took place, she was beginning to come apart at the seams. She started to use drugs at work, something she vowed she would never do out of concern for the children she taught. She recalls joking about the World Trade Tower collapse: "That's how emotionally hard I had become."

She had a disturbing nightmare about the towers coming down and children climbing stairs in the wrong direction. "I could see my mother all the way at the top. She was saying 'Run, Rosa, run.' And, 'This is the house of the Devil.' I saw this little light coming from the wall, and I started taking the wood out, trying to get the kids to go in. I woke up and started screaming. I went downstairs and started smoking like a chimney. That's when I knew that I couldn't hold it. I knew that I was going to end up in a mental hospital. My mom took care of me that whole night. I insisted on going to work to give my resignation before going to NLFG. I still wanted a good, how you say, reference, for other jobs. Everyone was so nice … . I wanted to be with the kids, but I couldn't handle it anymore. Life as I knew it didn't make sense to me."

She was having murderous thoughts but didn't tell her mother. Then her mother told her of a dream she had in which a person's face kept changing so that she couldn't tell who it was. In her mother's nightmare, Rosa murdered someone and went to jail.

"I knew then I would die unless I got help," Rosa says. "And when I got to New Life I knew that God was saving my life."

Rosa says she is reaching the point where she will be able to have healthy relationships. She adds that God recently impressed on her how much he loved her. This has always been a concern for her, feeling unloved. "So the answer to the identity question is that there are God-given gifts that I either, like, repressed or did not know about. I am in the process of discovering them now. And the static in my head is going away. God delivered me of the static."

In the second floor residents' lounge Rosa joins Liza, Holly, and Tawanda. Liza is a vegetarian and has practiced Buddhism in the past. "I eat lots of peanut butter sandwiches here!" Liza laughs. She laughs often. It is both an aspect of her fun-loving, easy-going nature and a distancing mechanism, a determination not to take anything here too seriously. She also thinks of her upbeat nature as a spiritual gift, a form of ministry. "I like to make people laugh," she grins, running her fingers through her cropped, sandy blonde hair.

After work period I receive the hoped-for invitation to someone's room, from Jade. Lily cryptically describes Jade as "a woman of many stripes." She seems aloof at times, yet seeks me out. Perhaps it is because she enjoys writing and thinks of me as a writer, a kindred spirit. In fact she was one of the first Dover residents to "reach out" to me. We sit on her bed talking about the concepts of community and community building.

Jade describes a vision of herself as a community builder and mentions the importance of the large community beyond New Life. She says it would not be possible to accomplish what NLFG accomplishes on an outpatient or day treatment basis. She bounces on the bed, eager to make her point. "With the secular programs there's not a family, a community. The atmosphere of a secular program is, you gotta get your life together and that's that. You know what I mean? You speak with a counselor or whatever, but your stuff is your stuff and yours alone. There is no bonding. Not like in here. This atmosphere is a family atmosphere. In a secular program you gotta put on the façade and get your act together. God doesn't allow that in here. After living with somebody for so long, eventually the stuff that they're trying to hide comes out. You know what I mean? Because I believe that the spirit, and the counseling, and the leadership, and the classes, and everything that goes on in here whether you like it or not makes your masks disappear. And the discernment and the wisdom of the leaders who are here—they say, 'No, that mask gotta go.' And if you choose to hold on to it, then you won't change.

"Once they see what's going on, they'll tell you to let go of it. But if you choose not to, you know, there's only so much they can do. It's almost like I get the desire to change 'cause they know it's not me. They know that it's a form of hiding pain and insecurities and stuff like that."

Jade pauses, fingering a computer-generated sketch of herself, her eyes half-closed, almost dreamlike. "What I'm about to do in the community is on the other side of being a community destroyer. When I was in the streets I was destroying—I brought down the community by my lifestyle. You know, by walking down the street and having cars pull over while I was walking down the street in front of people's houses where their kids were. Nobody wants to live in a community like that. Selling drugs right around the corner, down the street from good people. Nobody wants that type of person in their community. I mean, I wouldn't use near my home where my children were because I knew, even in my addiction, that I was destroying the area. But I didn't care about myself or the ghetto where I was doing it. I wouldn't use near my people, my family, but I'd go to someone else's community. I felt as though I destroyed not only myself but, you know, people's safety. Them seeing the prostitution, the drugs, you know, the cops riding around chasing everybody who does this stuff all day long around the community.

"But now the Lord has restored my life and I want to go back into the community and help. Help the people, help the girls who are out there, so that they're not out there no more."

She shakes her head. "So if I help the people, the women, and tell them that they ain't got to be there no more. *Your kids ain't got to see you no more down.* They'll get esteem in their selves and in God, hopefully. Then they won't want to be a mess no more. They won't let their yards be a mess where people ride by and their lawn be all muddy and their kids be all raggedy, hair uncombed, walking around outside in diapers. That's a lot of what the ghetto is, a reflection of poor self-esteem. With help they'll take care not only in their selves but in their education and their neighbors and what's going on with the neighborhood. What's going on in their homes, you know. And then it's a domino effect."

Jade leans forward, intensely earnest. "In most treatment programs I don't see the caring, I see finances. Money, money, money—the real sense of helping is gone. It's like, 'I'm paid, and I really don't want to hear about all these problems day after day.' Maybe that doesn't apply to a new person who just comes in, but after they've have been there for a few years the love and desire to help is gone. It becomes routine.

"I can say that because I've been in over ten programs, and it's always the same. In prison, they'll help people who are really, really pressing to get help. And they are aware of the power they have. See, they won't tell you that after so long you can get into a college while still in prison. They won't tell you the benefits of being in prison because then they have to pay for that. If you start to pass and you're good and not a troublemaker in prison, you can go through certain stuff, but most of the guards don't care. Some of them bring drugs in there and sell them to the girls. If inmates don't have money they trade it for sex. You know, if they are having a nicotine fit the guards will make them do … they'll degrade them. They'll strip … you know … . The guards will do stuff like spit on them, kick them, beat them, allow other girls to jump them. They'll even cover up if somebody's getting high in a cell. They'll allow women to have sex and cover for where they're supposed to be. And it's alright, as long as you ain't fighting."

She jumps to her feet and scoops up a picture of her daughter, repeating the hope that she will attend Brown University. Jade expresses her new calling in life: "I don't want to be judgmental towards anybody. I want to be able to socialize with the sophisticated, and I want to be able to relate to the bum on the street. The one who's so dirty that he looks like he has socks on but it's not socks, it's dirt. I want to be able to relate to him and be able to clean him up. Take him to my house and put him in my tub, because my tub is not too good for him. Put new clothes on him and feed him and then, you know, give him the word of God, at least plant a seed. I feel that how you treat people will come back to you, because God treated people all the same. The prostitute and the Pharisees, he treated them all the same. But some were open to him, and some weren't."

Later Jade trolls the hallway looking for takers for clothing she has to give away in preparation for her move to Rhode Island to go to college. She gives one person a sweater and gives someone else a microwave.

At dinner I am asked to pray. I take the opportunity to tell the whole group about my dream, the bowl filled with colorful gemstones, and that I understand the diamonds, emeralds, rubies, and sapphires to represent them. All the women in that long line around the cafeteria gaze at me in complete silence, taking this information in. Several times during the week I am asked to repeat the dream for someone who was not there to hear it firsthand.

I eat with Gisetta again, and Lupita. Gisetta has a long dark hair. Her thin face looks worried. She talks at length about her two sons, how they had to raise themselves while she was a single parent finishing college, then working full time and using drugs. She is now "dealing with guilt." Her mother's condemnation adds to her guilt: "I wonder why my sons even visit me." I tell her that children are very resilient; they could probably sense her love in spite of everything else. She responds quietly, "I receive that."

After dinner, fourteen women fill the van and head to a church

in York for a women's seminar. They are there at the invitation
of an alumna who is a church member. One of the women
on the bus is Laura from Fresno, soon to be twenty-one. In
two weeks she will return to California. Laura has pulled her
sunny blonde hair into a loose ponytail. Her cheeks dimple
when she talks. She says that her parents were addicts and it
fell to her to raise the young children of her mother and stepfather. Her parents have been sober and Christian for eight
years now. Standing firm in her role as a sibling, not a parent,
will be the biggest challenge for her (and her family).

The bus pulls up to the church where there is a lavish
reception: shrimp and fancy hors d'oeuvres, tables full of des-
serts and snacks. During the reception Sarah and Kenda take
offense at how some of the women in the church behave
toward them. "These women are guarding their purses," they
say, pointing to several older women huddled in a small group,
whispering to each other.

Worship is led by a spirited "girl band" with a country
western twang. They have a touching confidence and virtu-
osity. A young red-haired violinist plays several instruments
during the evening.

After the women return to Dover and are ready for bed,
there is a discussion about depression. As she finishes brushing her teeth, Jessie confesses she has dealt with depression
while at NLFG. Before the program she was diagnosed and
treated for bipolar disorder, but she had to be off her medication to enter the program. For a while she had highs and lows,
but, "They've balanced out now." She describes a capacity to
recognize the onset of a low pattern and "nip it in the bud."
Rosa mentions a similar capacity to notice the static in her
head. "I have to remind myself that's an old behavior," she
says. "Sometimes it's hard to distinguish what's old and what's
new." Jessie recalls a period in which she discovered herself: "I
would have these highs in worship or whatever and then go
into a low and doubt the legitimacy of the high. I'd ask, 'Was

that real, God?' Oh it was terrible." She thinks bipolar disorder was a misdiagnosis—"It was an emotional, not a mental problem"—and regards hers as a healing of emotions, not of mental illness.

Climbing into her bed, Jesse talks about her counseler role, which she describes as a listening process. "The biggest thing that I'm learning is how to be a good listener. I think that's one of the most important things. A lot of times people just need to talk things out. You can just listen and they'll just talk and talk and kind of work things out themselves and then they just feel better because they just release. It can be exhausting though. I have to be careful not to take on all those burdens. I make sure I just release them back to the Lord, pray for them, and then just put it in their hands, knowing that I can't do anything to change them. It's only going to be the Holy Spirit. I just spend time in prayer for them, and if the Lord leads me in any specific way or through Scripture to share with them, then fine. But just to be a good listener, I think that's real important. We come from a background of being addicts, alcoholics, whatever. We've anesthetized our feeling for all of our life. So now we're in these situations where we are feeling intense emotions, and sometimes that's very frightening; when that anger or fear flares up, it can be overwhelming. I think of James 5:16: Confess your sins or falter. Whatever you're going through, pray for each other so that you may be healed; that's the way the Lord has it designed. Sometimes we can just do it with God alone, but sometimes we need others in the body."

Jessie calls NLFG a place of continuous learning, where teachers and students are colearners, discovering common ground: "I'm so excited about teaching because through it I'm learning, I'm growing, I'm healing. As I learn from the students, they learn from me, and we learn from one another. We find out we're all the same. We might have different paths or different backgrounds, but deep inside we all need to feel like we belong and have value—that we're competent. When I read the ladies' comment sheets after class, they write things like, 'I found that I'm not crazy after all, or I'm not strange after all.' That's so important, because so often we feel that we're so different, and we're really not.

"The class meets Tuesdays and Thursdays. I told the students that every Thursday they would do a comment sheet. This is preparation for when they go downstairs to Omega, where I believe they must do a comment sheet for every class. I tell them it can be a comment on me, the subject, or a question they didn't want to ask in front of the other students, anything really. For the most part they just share with me what they have received from the class, what the Lord is speaking to them and how the Lord is ministering to them through it. It's great to hear their positive feedback. That, wow, they're really receiving healing, really being challenged, and they are growing. And it's all the glory to God, but if we're just willing to be used, he'll use you, you know."

Brooke knocks on the door and asks for the medicine closet key to get something for her cold. The "meds closet" is controlled by staff and accessed only at specific times of day. The key is in Jessie's room, so emergency cases knock on her door. Medicines must be alcohol-free. Jessie says the interruptions sometimes "wear on her."

She yawns and wishes her roommates a good night's rest.

TWELVE
BREATHE

Saturday, April 13, 2002

The early morning quiet is broken by Tyrone, Ursula's son, who comes into the bathroom while I am brushing my teeth. He shows interest in my laptop computer. His sister, Tayesha, joins our conversation. I invite both of them to my room to try doing some typing. They enjoy it. Considering the number of children it is amazing how peaceful the house is most of the time.

Today, residents pile into the van en route to the second day of a women's conference. Sue is a recent arrival from the Westminster center. She has been in the program once before and talks about how her family's needs pulled her out of the program prematurely, at level 1 of R & O: "I was pulled down by my husband, now my ex." This time she is determined to stay and complete the program. She has four children, between fourteen and eighteen. From Harford County originally, they moved to the city of Baltimore. When asked about her city experience, she says only, "Bad." She shakes her head. Drugs are not just an urban problem, she insists. Her son tells her that, in Harford, $5 bags of heroin and Ecstasy are available in tenth grade.

The women assemble at the locked front door of the church, early arrivals. They stand in a light drizzle on this cool morning, listening to a woodpecker. The women are not chosen to be here due to a reward or selection process but by process of elimination. These are all the women not in "blackout" (disciplines) or in the choir. Denise has a self-deprecating humor. Describing herself, she laughs over how another staffer, Lucia, (whose primary language is Spanish) gave her the nickname "birdmind," intending to say birdbrained, or absent-minded. In addition to alcohol, Denise began using marijuana at fourteen. "I watched TV all the time, yet I had no idea there were Christian programs," she says. One of the hosts arrives, smiling, to open the door for the group.

While waiting for the breakfast buffet, Denise and residents Luz and Hope talk. The seating at reception and breakfast is in informal circles, which encourage people to mix. Despite some diverse groupings, most women segregate according to their affiliation with New Life or the church. There are about sixty attendees, so NLFG represents a significant contingent with a dozen residents and two staffers.

Balancing a plate of food on her knees, Luz describes herself as feeble-minded and homeless when she entered NLFG five months earlier. She was diagnosed as schizophrenic and could not speak English. Prior to her homelessness and mental breakdown, she had been led to a house and gang-raped: "I was betrayed by a man from my church, one I thought was Christian." She remembers crying out during the rape, "Why did you betray me like this?" She was abandoned in a field outside the house where she was raped. She tried to kill herself with a knife, but someone held her and prevented her from doing it. She wonders aloud, "Was it the man, or was it Christ? Was I hallucinating?" She wound up living in a trailer box from an old semi, which is where her family found her. Luz chose NLFG from a short list, supplied by a social worker, who helped get her into the program. Two of her three sons are with her. One son is still on the street; she is trying to locate him and get him to NLFG. When she was discovered in the box, she kept rocking back and forth, saying, "Sanctuary, sanctuary," a kind of catatonic prayer. She believes that God led her to NLFG, her "sanctuary." Everyone at the table sits engrossed in her story when an event hostess says loudly, "Time to gather in the sanctuary!" The women chuckle in surprise at the coincidence. As they file into the meeting space, Luz says she has forgiven her rapists. Recently, someone prophesied to her that she would preach to the world.

Hope, from Chicago, was also homeless. A pastor helped her get into the Westminster introduction center (there were no openings in Chicago). She had no money of her own, she admits. "I was blessed exceedingly." Hope describes herself as quiet and says that, for her, communication requires trust. She has been gradually opening up to other women in the program. "Why are we considered not rooted, unless we have a home?" she wonders. "Why does mobility make us so uncomfortable?" She is forming answers to her own questions, puzzling through the spiritual implications of lifestyle choices she will be making after NLFG.

A casual observer would never guess these women had lived on the streets under such profoundly disabling conditions. They are articulate. They appear well and "normal."

During the large-group session the speaker says that God is a God of order, therefore believers should have orderly lives. She cites Genesis 2, the creation story. The topic seems as appropriate for NLFG as for the regular church members. The speaker also talks about the importance of praising God when requesting healing (Luke 13:10) and knowing when to relinquish control (Proverbs 31).

The speakers—who have referred to their own experiences with physical and sexual abuse, marital or childrearing problems, and substance abuse—have created a setting with potential for shared meaning.

During breaks several residents and staffers have asked if I'm having fun. They mean visiting New Life, not just the seminar. The question surprises me at first. I say, "It must look as if I'm having fun." Jessie confirms this. I add that I am enjoying being with them and ask if they "enjoy" the program. Their answers differ according to each individual's experiences, yet they all talk about experiencing "joy." These conversations remind me that I am bridging groups: NLFG and the church women of the larger community. I am perceived as part of both, yet not entirely: a hybrid. The New Life community has adopted me as an insider, even though its members are well aware that my experiences and conditions of membership are not the same as theirs. The church women see me as a member of the NLFG community by my willing association.

The presenter for the first small-group session says she used to volunteer at the NLFG children's home in Glen Rock and was impressed by the spirit of cooperation she observed there. When the speaker mentions that in individual lives "the power of Christ is made perfect in weakness" (II Corinthians 12:9–10), Bess excitedly highlights the verse, already underlined in pen in her Bible, whispering, "These verses were prophesied over me!"

The day's final speaker teaches a lesson based on First Peter, Chapter 2, exhorting listeners to build up each other and the kingdom of God. She reminds everyone that we are "living stones, as Christ is" and elaborates, "You are gemstones!" NLFG women glance at each other and smile, nodding their heads at the familiar metaphor. On the bus ride back to NLFG the gemstone coincidence is a topic of lively conversation. But something the director says on Sunday will bring a whole new meaning to the image.

The women return to Dover in time for the evening meal. After dinner, Rosa reads aloud a letter from a former coworker in Philadelphia, telling her she is loved, and encouraging her. The letter references the "demons within us" (referring to the two of them) but also remarks: "God doesn't make no junk." Rosa explains: "My friend has five children but was curious about the lesbian lifestyle. She told me she wanted to experiment, but I warned her off. I said to her, 'Once you get into it how do you know you will be able to get out?'" Her point is that on some level they both considered the lifestyle wrong (Rosa uses the phrase, "of the devil"). Rosa has changed considerably. She is more peaceful. She also seems more reticent, but this is her real personality, she says. Interestingly, even though the angry Rosa was all about projecting strength, she exudes it now.

Jessie clowns in the hallway with an R&O junior staff member named Deirdre. They are at opposite ends of the hall, singing messages to each other in operatic (Jessie) and falsetto (Deirdre) voices. As residents arrive for evening chapel, some women are peering out the window, waving as Anabelle's family leaves. (One spectator grins, explaining, "Cute brother!")

During chapel Jade invites the women to choose someone to bless. "Bless someone who has not already been blessed." She instructs a number of the women to bless their "sandpaper sisters." Kenda, as at Westminster, is sensitive to people's needs. She blesses Sarah, "who needs encouragement right now. Being a mom with a baby here is tough." After blessings everyone participates in a round of hugs.

At snack, Jessie expresses concern about whether Iris will stay. She asks Iris, "How is it going?" Laughing uneasily, Iris tells her story in a nutshell. "I'm different. I don't have a substance abuse problem, and I don't have to stay here. But God wanted me to stay here once, I said 'No,' and things just started falling apart." She is from Iowa and came here straight from three years in prison; her family does not know she is here and her son is in a mental health institution. The big, impossing woman reeled off stories of violence and tragedy without blinking an eye.

The women go to their rooms to get ready for bed.

Almost as soon as she climbs into bed, Shasta falls sound asleep, gently snoring. Jessie speaks proudly of a video her older brother made for her at Christmas. Her family is close, very affectionate. She says that her older brother is now the only nonbeliever in the family, the rest having come to faith as adults. "He is living a gay lifestyle." she adds. She is here with her family's support, even her mother's, who was controlling ("but God spoke to my mother about it and she's much better now"). She is one of the women at the R&O stage who signed a paper committing to the ministry for an additional six months. Those who do receive a 4-day pass. That practice might appear cultlike to some—and it would be, if there were no choice, or no written, mutually accepted terms. The six months serve as a transition period during which women are observed and encouraged in the areas in which they need further development.

Jessie witnessed her mom's abuse at the hands of an alcoholic father, which has made it difficult for her to trust and receive her husband's affection. She also says her early relationship with her father did not always have "good boundaries."

The choir returns around midnight. They performed at Friday and Saturday night meetings and have two more performances tomorrow. Elsa excitedly explains that the speaker at a chapel in Hummelstown confirmed an earlier prophecy for her saying, "You will reach nations upon nations." She is an evangelist with a heart desire to travel, she claims. But in the past, relapse kept her from fulfilling the prophecy. She prays that everyone will be able to get back to sleep.

But I can't sleep. So I go to the lounge to write field notes. I talk to Deirdre, who's on night duty. She came through Westminster and has been here sixteen months. Deirdre is R&O 4 and will graduate in April. She is petite and athletic looking, with sleek blonde hair that reaches the middle of her back and dimples that appear when she smiles, which is almost always. "I was just three credits shy of graduating from college when I entered New Life. I prided myself on academic performance—until my grades fell because of my partying. For me, the hard part was the condemnation, that sense of failure." She pauses. "You know, what we experience here is a like a lifetime of learning condensed into a short time." She is reading Mere Christianity. *We talk about C.S. Lewis until 2:00 a.m.*

THIRTEEN
HEART OF STONE

Sunday, April 14, 2002

Rules are posted on a bulletin board in the cafeteria hallway. One posting shows program levels and who is at each level while another describes levels of privilege and restrictions and who is at each level. A third posting lists the classes and teachers, and a fourth gives guidelines for book reports. To an outsider they would seem terse, cryptic.

GROUP PRIVILEGES AND RESTRICTIONS
Groups A–C
Each letter represents two additional disciplines.

Mail:
    A: Four out, unlimited in
    B: Three out, unlimited in
    C: None in or out
Phone:
    A: Three in during month; two out or in between 15th
        and 29th
    B: Two in, one out
    C: None in or out
Visits:
    A: Three during month; allowed out two of three
    B: Two in; one out
    C: None in or out
Shopping/other trips/visiting homes/babysitting:
    A: Chosen first
    B: Chosen if room
    C: None

Tape players, Walkmans:
    A: W.M. weekdays after five, weekends tape players
    B. W.M, players from 5 p.m. Fri–Mon 9:30 a.m.
    C. No music
Choir:
    A: Chosen first, especially trips out of town
    B: May be chosen
    C. No music
Working for money:
    A. First as in need
    B. Chosen if specific need
    C. Not allowed
Classes:
    Alpha:
      Motherhood (Osage) Daily 8-9
      Relationships (Jessie) Tue, Thur 9-11
      Growing up Spiritually (Denise) Wed, Fri 9-11
    Omega:
      Cults and Errors (Marilyn) Daily 8-9
      Emotional and Spiritual Power (Dianna, Tue,
        Thurs 9-11)
      Leadership (Carlos) Wed, Fri 9-11
      Lupita (Study Hall)

    Omega I:
    Tawanda, Holly, Brooke
    Omega II:
    Sarah
    Omega III:
    Gisetta, Kenda, Martee, Lupita

BOOK REPORT FORMAT
Books, 100 pages plus
    Cover, about author, main idea, spiritual truth,
      recommendation, due last Wednesday of each month

Breakfast starts at 8:30 sharp. On this morning in the Joy lounge, Etta's preschool-aged daughter Quantelle sits in a high chair eating breakfast. She is all smiles and says a few shy words. Ursula's children, Tayeesha and Tyrone, pop in to say hi before they go off to school. The lounge serves as a social transition space for residents.

Inez is one of the women in the lounge helping out even as she gets ready for the day. She is a serious, physically imposing woman who might be intimidating except that her eyes and manner are gentle. She has a son, twenty, and a daughter, sixteen. Inez is giddy that they are coming for her graduation. Her mother raised her children.

"The worst thing of living your life is not knowing your purpose or destiny. Why do I have to sleep with my stepfather? Why do I have to live on the streets? Why do I have to *live?*" She says she thought life was about dying—"I thought I would die a prostitute, a crackhead. Die on the railroad tracks. Everything in the world is so temporary. Now I've got a hold of a light beam, an eternal purpose. Our purpose is all about relationship," she says, meaning with God and others. She looks up a verse in the Bible. "Even animals have a longing to be loved." She reads aloud Matthew 19:29: "And every one that hath forsaken houses, or brethren, or sisters, or father, or mother, or wife, or children, or lands, for my name's sake, shall receive a hundredfold, and shall inherit everlasting life." She interprets: "God is saying, 'I'm asking you to put me first. Love me more than you love your children.'"

The connection between God's love and her purpose is very important to Inez. What sounds at first like biblical permission to neglect home and family is to Inez an entirely new way to love, live, and *create* a home and family. "I learned about Christian programs from a cellmate. I learned about NLFG from a pastor whose niece is [NLFG staffer] Marilyn." Inez continues: "I want to serve the Lord, with all of my heart. I

told God, 'If you restore my life I will go to the far corners of
the earth for you.'"

CeCe, Bess, and Hope gather in the second-floor lounge
in Love Hall prior to chapel. Similar to the other lounges, this
one has a table and a well worn assortment of mismatched
chairs. All three women arrived here from the Chicago introduction center, and are friends. In fact, probably the biggest
influence on formation of friendships here is having jour-
neyed through the same introduction center together. CeCe
teases Hope about studying all the time and calls her "teacher."
Hope says quietly, "Other people have asked me whether I
am a teacher. I wonder what people see in me? Now I see
myself so differently from my homeless self." Hope shows off
pictures of her two sons. The elder is thirteen. "Last month
Lily arranged a surprise visit. When I saw my son, I cried."
Hope came to Dover two months ago. In her soft voice she
observes, "It took two weeks to get adjusted, to figure out
who I could trust. At first, I didn't talk to anyone."

Bess arrived Easter Sunday. It is her second time at NLFG
and she remembers having to beg to get in the first time. The
Chicago director gave each woman at the intro center a rag
doll to illustrate different personality traits. CeCe chimes in,
"Yeah, she told me, 'You're pulled this way and that way.' I
didn't know how to take that." Hope laughs and says, "She
gave me a little doll and said, 'You take little steps.' That's true.
I used to live for the next drink." Bess and Hope speak in
one voice about their journeys to New Life. Bess says, "I was
tired of being tired." Hope adds, "That's right. Tired of being
tired. Time to surrender." Bess continues, "I surrendered in
September 1994. Also gave my kids to God." When she found
herself on the verge of relapse, she recalls thinking, "I've got
to go home," meaning NLFG. "They called me. I had my excuse: a court date in April. But Brother James said, 'I'm going
to call the director. Me and the director is coming to get you.'
I've heard stories about them going to dope houses. Worse

than the cops coming is the thought of Brother James and
the director finding me in some crack house. That would be
so humiliating."

NLFG is more than "a program" to residents. Hope states
emphatically: "This is not a cult, and it's not a program. New
Life is a ministry. We are not being programmed. And it has
to be residential—to grow and to be taken out of the world—
daily living and habits are a distraction."

Bess chimes in: "It is so different from other programs
I been in. You won't be needing no cigarettes here. A lot of
people can't comprehend that, even though they see a difference." The difference, Hope says—and the surprise—for her
was the intimate nature of the God-relationship: "God actually talks to you through his Word! That's the thing that gets
me the most: God predestined this place and planned everything—to prepare me!"

Following a walk outside to enjoy a breezy spring day,
women enter the chapel by a side door and take a seat for the
service. Jessie asks everyone to move up closer. This seems to
break the ice and generate quiet conversation and laughter.

The director's message is based on John 6:16–41. His point
is that God is not capricious. He mentions Mae, an alumna
who is now a highly placed probation officer in charge of
youth offenders. Another alumna is head of personnel at a
university. "Programs deal with the physical, psychological
part of man. Not the spiritual part. Hell will be full of some
very healthy people. Jesus came to transform us, not reform us.
They tried to reform me at Rikers Island. But there was nothing to reform. We're sinful. We have to be transformed by the
renewing of our minds. We need to feed on the Word. Op-
erating on your own will alone opens the door to the devil
bringing junk to your mind. It's not just superficial. You've
been transformed.

God did not come to repair, he came to replace. He has
given you a heart of flesh to replace a heart of stone. Now

you will be able to love, have compassion. Ephesians 2:5 says
we are sinful from conception. Romans 7:14–25 says I want
to do right but can't. I go to a program and stay clean for a
while. Who's going to deliver me—the environment? Some
psychologist? John 10:10 says the thief comes to steal, destroy
… Jesus came to bring life more abundantly. A heart of flesh
for a heart of stone. Live life with your new heart. Then you
can make phone calls to me and say, 'I'm a probation officer
… I'm head of personnel.'"

*The heart of stone image resonates with my gemstones dream. Both
describe a radical transformation of the whole woman—formerly
society's rubble, now highly valued. Such change is not humanly
possible.*

A guest at chapel is a student from Youth Challenge Bible
Institute in Sunbury, Pennsylvania. The informal web of faith-
based programs of which NLFG is a part creates many op-
portunities for networking.

Opal, the keyboardist, seamlessly segues from one song to
another. She uses the lyrics, "Take me back Lord to the place
where I first received you" to illustrate reconciliation in her
life. "I'm going to be a pastor," she says. "Yet my own mother
gave up on me: 'You will never amount to anything' she told
me. That was a lie from the pit of hell!"

Among today's prayer requests are healings for the Dover
director, who has a double hernia, and the Westminster director, who has hepatitis C. (Later in the month we hear they
both received clean bills of health.)

*Lily gives me a list of alumnae after the service. She does not know
what they are currently doing but checked off the names of those who
graduated more than two years ago. I will also try to contact the two
alumnae the director mentioned in his sermon. Lily makes a pouting*

face when I tell them that I'm leaving Tuesday night and says, "We'll miss you."

At mealtime, Patti finds a place to sit. Tawanda sees her and sits across the room. She says, "We're not really talking—we give each other a lot of space. We're too much alike. I have strong opinions, you know." Patti does her best to avoid eye contact.

Sarah, Bess, Rosa, and Ruth pull up chairs. The conversation turns to the subjects of babies, moms, and bonding. Sarah worries about whether her baby will bond with too many people, "Can Lea have too many moms?" she wonders. Everybody says no, this experience is good for her. At NLFG, the daycare makes it possible for moms to fully participate in classwork, work schedule, and some extracurriculars but still be available to their children. Lea is a happy, alert, social baby. That more or less describes all of the children at NLFG. Some of the visiting children are a different story. Holly's son Bradley and Brooke's son Casey come to mind. They seem chronically fussy, angry, and distracted. Sarah says, "It's hard for me to keep up with homework, really hard. But I appreciate the structure of the program and the opportunity to have my baby with me."

After lunch some women take up an invitation from the director and Carlos to go on a "hike." The weather looks threatening, but a handful are game. The director drives a smaller van, accompanied by Mark, a part-time staffer. Carlos drives the larger van. Both Carlos and Mark are among the few male graduates of NLFG. They follow the director in drizzling rain. Birdsong can be heard through an open window, with snatches of song and the constant hum of conversation going on inside the van. The vans travel through green valleys veiled in mist—hauntingly beautiful, though the chances for a hike do not seem too promising.

Carlos talks about his past in Hawaii while he drives. He is a former Marine. So is Jolane, who sits nearby. She says wryly, "I tried lots of things to get off drugs, including the Marines." She has an athletic build, a disciplined manner, and holds herself with straight-backed dignity. There is something else: sadness, wounded pride, perhaps. Carlos left the Marines because his habit got hard to hide. "There is no double jeopardy immunity—the military would punish drug use and also allow the civil courts to punish the drug use. My friends were either dying or getting caught." For a while he sold cars in Hawaii. He tells a funny story about "wiping out" at a Taco Bell drive-in lane on a moped while under the influence. "You know, that's pretty hard to do," he grins. The sobering message: He was out of control.

"At first I missed Hawaii, but I knew I could not return. One friend was shot and killed. Another was sent to prison for twenty years. Everyone said, 'Carlos, you're next.'" He came to NLFG right off the streets.

The vans pull into Rocky Ridge Park. It's no longer raining, but the park closes in about an hour. The band of "hikers" walks to an overlook, then loops back through a playground. At the overlook they line up at the railing to take in the view. One side of the horizon is engulfed by dark, foreboding storm clouds and jags of lightning, and the other side is transformed by sunlight breaking through: a spiritual metaphor in the sky.

Some of the mothers and children play on the rocks below. The director has a camera and snaps pictures. Rosa won't come over to the railing because she's afraid of heights, so she sticks to the trail just off the deck platform.

Back in the van, everyone seems to have a silly joke to tell, even the children. Carlos talks about trying moments in ministry. He says he has no mechanical ability or experience, yet maintenance is his primary responsibility at NLFG. "Growing up in New York City, I learned from my father the secret to fixing things: 'Call the Super.' Once, an underground water pipe to the dormitory broke, and I could not find the leak. I had to dig for it along and under the road, then struggle to repair it. James talked me through it on the phone. It took me four days. We were without water for most of the time. The second time it happened, it took two days. Third time, two hours." Another pipe leak stymied him. "Then I recalled the theme from a Bible study: Listen to God. I listened at the back of the house, and followed the sound of water to the leak. These moments built patience in me. One day my son was watching me repair something and he said, 'Wow, you have so much patience. I'd be hurling the thing by now!' God uses moments like these to build up our spiritual capabilities."

One resident is teaching another some words in sign language. The sign for "God" is especially interesting: palm flat and hand drawn down the center of your face.

I hear Rosa say I look "whiter." When I look at my skin, she clarifies, "No I said 'wider.'" I joke about this comment. Kenda gets in on it too: "Walk on the wide side."... "Did the director take a picture of your wide side?" After more teasing Rosa says, "I'm sorry. I didn't mean to say that, but you know I can only tell the truth to you."

FOURTEEN
DOUBLE DUTCH

Monday, April 15, 2002

I wake up at 6:30 to birdsong and snoring. The swag curtains billow in the breeze coming through the open window. They are sheer and have a delicate pattern of flower buds and fan-shaped leaves. Transparency and light. There are no hiding places.

I go outside during work period but do not volunteer to help. This is the first time I have sought a private moment for reflection. From the woods emanates a rich chorus of birdsong, punctuated by a woodpecker. I also hear the distinctive cooing of a mourning dove and the rarer, more musical voice of an oriole. I walk to the playground, wipe dew off the end of the sliding board, and sit down. Stray clouds trim the edge of a blue sky. Behind me I hear voices, children and women and the staccato of a basketball. Inez had mentioned double dutch jump rope later. The sun warms my face and forearms. I am facing south. A screen of trees buffers the campus— "mountain" is what they say here—from the road and the larger world, though I can hear cars go by.

Based on the women's experiences with multiple treatment programs, I hypothesize a treatment and recovery continuum defined by a person's readiness to learn and change, and therefore different for each individual. As human beings we can learn from every life experience, therefore multiple programs (if positive in some way) can have a positive cumulative effect, as the individual sees what works, what doesn't, and why. This hypothesis fits comfortably with the New Life model, which affirms the uniqueness of each student. However, a continuum based on readiness calls into question "one-size-fits-all" treatment models, models which are involuntary, and those which absolve addicts from the responsibility to change or consider them incapable of changing, because addiction is viewed as a disease or a genetic predisposition.

Underlying the New Life approach is the importance of getting out of the old setting to remain clean and sober. The program recognizes the chaos of street and prison life, where people become objects, and the primary lessons are how to manipulate people and work the system to one's advantage. "Boot camp" therapeutic communities are not seen as lasting solutions by residents who have experienced them because they do not address deeper issues or allow for identity change. The key is not the program but the faith enrichment, or as an NLFG alumna puts it: "The program was not my savior. It introduced me *to* the Savior. This morning Shasta is cheerful and talkative, but Jessie is quiet. Part of the conversation last night was about privacy. People are constantly coming into Jessie and Shasta's room for keys to the exterior doors or medicine cabinet. They knock and then come right in, so it feels as if there's no private space. They have had "key" room duties for three months and have grown weary of it. Last night, there were at least six interruptions. Jessie says she finally "flipped out" over the issue early this morning. She is hoping to move to a single room, perhaps Jade's or Ursula's.

Rosa has been thinking about the deeper meanings of her experiences and outdoors, at free time, wants to talk about this. "There are women who come here feeling ignored and insignificant. That nothing about them will change. I was like, man, God is awesome because through this research that Michele's doing, even though she's using fictitious names, we know deep inside that we've touched whoever is going to read it with our stories. And God in his own tender way has exalted us. Like the resident, Luz, she was out there homeless, you know how bad that had to be? Feelin' like nobody, she was just there, but not there, like invisible, you know what I am saying? And I think of my own self being ignored, put away, and still wanting somebody. Being insignificant. And God does this healing—I feel it's healing and not in a selfish way, but glorifying him. I didn't even see that until now." Rosa gestures to her heart. "It gets me right here, it touches me."

She sits on the sandbox, fiddling in the sand with a toy shovel the children have left behind. Rosa likens her identity confusion to putting on an act: "I used to feel like I was on stage all of the time. I didn't know how to be myself anymore. I was one way at home—the daughter, the mother. But I didn't feel like a mother to my own daughter. When I was at the bar I was anything you wanted me to be. I'm so grateful that God is helping me find out who I truly am. I can't live the way I lived. I can't do that because I know I would lose myself all over again. Thank God for my sound mind, for the restoration of my daughter. I just want God to fulfill my heart in every way. He's given me a new identity, and today I can sit here and say that he has loved me through my confusion."

She talks about her first impressions of the introduction center. Rosa enjoyed the intimacy of Westminster and felt lonely when she transitioned to the much larger population at Dover. "I think God knows what he is doing with this whole program. When you come off the street you are so messed up. I mean the one thing that really got to me, that won me over, was the way that they treated the girls and the way they treated me. Even when they rebuke you there was so much love. Then when you come here it's totally the opposite. But what they are teaching you here is not the intimacy you need with other people but the intimacy you need with God. I have to say, God is a trip, man."

The distant sound of children having fun at the playground underscores her words. Rosa pauses before continuing, "My whole life was falling apart. I couldn't do school because I was drinking so much. College was too much of a hassle when I could just be relaxing. I got involved with this woman—I lusted her so bad. The fact that I was a big fat liar didn't make it better either. When I got with this woman and I opened up my friendship to her, she ended up starting to go to the bar a lot, too. I wanted her, but I didn't want any of the guys to want her. I got real territorial, and I kind of just let all the guys think that she was my lover. The fact that she was very affectionate and very lonely and she was going through this big thing with her best friend who stole her husband, that was messing her up. We ended up spending a lot of time together. I spent nights at her house and she spent nights at mine.

"And I was experimenting with this guy, the bartender. Mostly because she encouraged me. She would say, 'You're not gay.' I would say, 'You don't know, okay.' So I started experimenting with this guy, but that didn't stop me from wanting her. And the fact that she was very affectionate added to the fire. The guys there did not even try to get on her. I was really jealous and nasty. I liked that: I felt I had some control. My friend played along with it. She said, 'I really don't care.' She was a boxer, a kick boxer. She wasn't scared of anything. Me, I cared what everybody thought. My reputation was the biggest thing to me. That's how my life started crumbling. When I started messing with that man he ended up messing with me. She just kept encouraging me, all that time. They ended up together, and she found out that everybody really thought she was my lover. That's when we became enemies. It was terrible.

"When I found out they were going together that really hurt me because of my pride. I told her, 'This is exactly what I was talking about. Men are dogs. They will be with your best friend, mess with you, dump you, then leave you. I shut her up—that was my way of dealing with the hurt. All the time it was killing me inside. I never wanted him. I used to say that the only way a man could get me into bed was if he raped or beat me. And so the worst way for her to hurt me was to take my man. There was this one song with lyrics that went something like, 'Because inside you're ugly, ugly like me/ Now lay down on my bed, putting this cocaine through my veins.' This was something we would sing to each other—she would harass me like that. For a while I felt I was winning the battle, this ice-cold battle. That's when she ended up doing what she did."

Rosa picks a blade of grass and considers it as she gathers her thoughts. "She kept ringing the doorbell and calling me, saying, 'Rosa, come to the bar tonight.' I said I didn't have money, she said she would treat. Before leaving I remember this thing inside me saying, 'Don't go, don't go.' But I hardened my heart, my pride got to me. For some reason the bar was real bright, I didn't have a shot yet, and yet everything was very, very bright. They were already drunk. She said her guy wanted to give me a shot. I refused. She said, 'Why are you acting this way?' That's when I went off. I said, 'All men are dogs. They're home-Gs.' She said, 'We're going outside now.' When she turned, I hit her. We started fighting. She called friends from another bar. They asked if I hit her first, and I lied. I knew that they would beat me, which they did.

"They must have put something in my drink, because I couldn't move, I couldn't do anything." Rosa describes being taken to a back room where she was brutally raped. "When I went back in the bar they were mocking me. I was still sober. That's when I had my breakdown. That night, my Mom called from Florida. I was crying, and I didn't tell her what happened, but she kept trying to talk to me about the Lord. I said, 'I don't want you to talk to me about the Lord; I just need you to hear me.' I was so hurt.

"When I was sober I felt the pain. I couldn't deal with all that crazy emotion, the betrayal, losing my job, my pride, all of that." Rosa goes back to the subject of Westminster. "I didn't deny my sexual preference when I first entered New Life. Actually, I boasted about it and didn't care what anybody else thought. It was maybe a year and a half before that when I'd come out of the closet, so I was very happy about that. And when I came to Westminster, I did boast a lot about it. They didn't condemn me or anything like that, even though I went in with my walls up already. See, I didn't turn to that lifestyle, that gay lifestyle, until after I got saved the first time.

"This was when I was with a Christian man who was married to two women at the same time. That hurt me, but before that I was already struggling. I've struggled with my sexual preference since I was a little girl. I had to sneak around and do whatever, kissing in the bathroom or touching or whatever, but somehow when I came to be around twelve or thirteen the idea of being a lesbian was one of the worst things. I was afraid I was gonna go to hell. So I grew out of that phase thinking it was little kids' stuff. When I came into New Life they didn't condemn me or anything like that. They taught me that sin is sin no matter what it was. There's not bigger sin or smaller sin. The day that I decided to be a gay woman was also the day I decided to rebel against God. I was doing it more out of rebellion. That seed was in me already, having that sexual urge, being attracted to women and this and that. Once I started that lifestyle, which is like a whole culture in itself, then I started thinking, yeah, it's alright for me to be like this."

Rosa slowly shakes her head. "At first, I didn't talk about it much at Westminster because nobody was going to change me, so to me that wasn't the problem. To me my problem was alcohol. So when the gay issue popped up, which was one of the last things I started dealing with, they went through the Bible and made it clear what the Bible said—that sin is sin. Then they just kind of answered my question, 'If sin is sin, why did I feel like this when I was a little girl?' They answered a lot of my questions. Even when I was living that lifestyle, sometimes I would be caught in an intimacy that felt so wrong, and I was like, 'Why do I feel so wrong if it feels alright?' It was something only God could say. At New Life it's not brainwashing because they give you a choice. I had the choice, and I left Dover. I went back to my lover and didn't even want her. And it wasn't because I felt all dirty; it was because I didn't want it. I didn't want it because it hit me: It's all deception. When the truth hits you, all that deception starts going away. That's the freedom in it. It's the truth that is cleaning you out. That's why I came back to NLFG."

Her thoughts turn to her newfound freedom.

"Well, the only truth that you can have is through God, through the Word. How is it that I feel so free in God? When I came in here I was thinking that all of my life I've been controlled—physically, mentally verbally—in everything. In God somehow I have freedom. God is giving me freedom even though I am a slave to him."

When Rosa left Dover and went back to her partner, "It didn't work out," she said, "because I realized that it was what truth had set in my heart. Codependency had a lot to do with that relationship. So at that moment when I was hurt, I was hurt because I was hurting her. When I left Dover I saw everything through different eyes. I wasn't leaving my lover when I left her, I was leaving my friend and I was leaving a decent person." Rosa begins to cry. "Sometimes I think that one day I'll be able to restore that. I hope and pray that one day she will have the hope and peace I have found."

Rosa brushes the grass off her clothing and walks quietly for a minute. She observes that, although there are residents who try to scam the NLFG system, they eventually discover they are only hurting themselves. "At Westminster they can get away with breaking the rules sometimes because staff is not always on the floor at that moment. But then as time goes by the Holy Spirit starts working on you, starts giving you discernment. It had come to a point during intro where there wasn't any touching, where there wasn't any cursing, and where there wasn't any talking of our past; that was developed through the Holy Spirit. The rules are there, and yes you can get away with it because you're just off the street, but the more you surrender to God ... .You're following the rules and you're not even doing it because of the rules any- more. You're doing it because you feel good about yourself and you're pleasing God. It was a very good group. And it wasn't even about the group.

"But there was one thing I had a lot of trouble with—gos- sip. With gossip I felt like I was lying because even though I wasn't a part of it, even though I was only receiving it—lis- tening—I felt like I was involved in deception. You can't really get away with it; I can't get away with it. I tried to get away with a couple of things in there and got caught. One of my lovers used to call and say she was my mom. I wouldn't try that now. I'd be like, 'No, *I don't want nothing to do with that.*'" She waves her arms emphatically and laughs. "Not out of fear of getting caught, but just, God knows me."

The noon hour brings devotions, followed by study and free time. Tawanda tells me she would like to talk. We go to her room. Tawanda offers me a pillow to prop against a room- mate's bed so that I can sit comfortably on the floor. Tawa- nda stretches out on her bed, reflecting on how community works at New Life.

"I know this is a real community, where even though they have a different opinion about things, when push comes to shove, everybody pitches in and helps with babies, with homework. When I first came up here, I couldn't read. I could read a little bit, but my vocabulary, I mean I couldn't spell the words or put them together, but I could pronounce some of the words.

"All the girls pitched in. They always encouraged me, they always did, and I would just cry. There were a lot of nights when I first came to the program that I would just cry. I went from a D student to an A and B student. I can't study with the ladies because they have their own technique and it distracts me. They can say their memory verses out loud to each other, but I can't. I go in the bathroom and read them off a card and say them out loud."

Before she came to New Life, Tawanda relied on male relationships. "After my aunt had died I was living with my cousin. I couldn't take her kids; they were stealing my stuff, and I was getting violent. I started taking acid. Then I met this pimp, though I didn't know he was a pimp, He had this girl take me outside to turn tricks. A real nice man, he picked me up. I said if you're going to have some of this, take me back to Chicago. I was a long way from home. He took me back and said, 'I better never catch you out here again.' Sure did. Nice white man. Moved back to my family, lived with my mother's ex-landlord. I had a boyfriend who liked to fight too much. I never had no one boyfriend—always been in a couple. The ex-landlord, a paraplegic, was real nice to me. He said, 'You can have men's company, but they can't spend the night.' That was cool with me. I would sleep for two days, and he would never know I was in the house unless he come up to the door, 'cause I was tired from partying for a few days. Or I would smoke happy stick—marijuana dipped in embalming fluid—something with PCP on it.

"I had messed up my money and had nowhere to go when I met another man. We lived together for six months or so; I slept on the couch, and there was no sexual contact. I would cook for him before he went to work, and he gave me money for cigarettes. I initiated the sexual relationship and slept with him, but he didn't bother me at all. I had my boundaries when it came to sex: I wasn't into the prostitution thing. So I took the initiative. We got my clothes, and I moved in. I stayed with him fourteen years but had other relationships, and abuse came in. I didn't mind going to work now and again, but I would have to pay this bill, that bill; we started arguing about money. I started messing around, and he did too, I think. Eventually, I left. He remarried."

Tawanda has had a variety of jobs. "I distributed food at the foodbank. Registered voters. Worked at the Veteran's Administration office. Financial aid. That's where I learned about data entry. I liked that job. I went through public aid. All the jobs I had I went through public aid assistance. I've been able to work, but the drinking—I just couldn't think unless I had a drink."

Tawanda shifted to the edge of her bed, a grin spreading on her face. "Now I'll tell you about coming to New Life. I wanted to get out so bad. I was sick, literally sick. I needed a drink. When you're coming down from being drunk so long, you have a hangover. I stayed in a hotel when I had money or in a shelter when I didn't. I went to a guy I knew; I called him my pastor, my confessor, because he had talked to me about getting me into New Life. He brought me to the introduction center in Chicago. When the director asked me, 'Why do you want to come to New Life?' I broke down and told her I was going to die on the streets." Tawanda shakes her head. "I didn't want to die."

Staff member "Miss" Denise tends her garden in the evenings after dinner time. In the converted trailer she shares with Marilyn and Illana, the combined living room and dining areas are cozy, comfortable, and lived-in. Bric-a-brac fills the eye. Outside she has created a pretty space of flowers and a vegetable garden, fenced to protect the plants from deer. She gets excited about each day's new growth. Denise hand tilled, fertilized, and planted much of it from seed. She points out Lily's house next door, also a converted trailer. Lily also likes to garden and has colorfully landscaped the property. Denise points out dandelions growing through the macadam. "When I first came here those dandelions spoke volumes to me spiritually. That God can pierce through our stony hearts."

At the basketball court women are jumping double dutch with the clothesline Tawanda bought at the mall. Holly watches from a plastic lawn chair, surrounded by the carefree sounds of the playground in the distance. Holly leans back in her chair and smiles. "I think that NLFG is a big family. You can come here for healing and deliverance, but also you can make lifelong friends. Christian friendships. When I first got here, I wasn't too much into this place, but now that I've been here for awhile I think it's important to anyone who is trying to get up from an unsafe place to come here. Because this is an atmosphere of love and caring. You can just really seek God and faith on this mountain."

With the earnestness of a learner eager to please, Holly connects community building with her desire to evangelize. "I think being a community builder is important for yourself and for others, because once you're able to get out on your own and leave here then you are able to take that community building to other places. Other people will see that, and they will want the same community building that you have. I have friends back home who I want to share the community building with. I want to share the gospel, and hopefully they can turn my community building into their building."

Holly watches the double dutch. She and the other spectators jokingly call the proceedings, "Double Dutch Olympics." There is an element of competition, but it's different from the usual win-lose competition in other games. The women who have the most consecutive jumps are aware of the numbers and their relative position, yet everyone is encouraged to try, and keep trying, until they successfully achieve the jump. Iris garners cheers when she breaks thirty jumps. Jessie approaches the ropes cautiously, protesting she's never jumped rope before. She quizzes the rope turners about the correct point of entry.

Double dutch jump rope is a girl's game, a school playground and street game. It requires team effort and coordination. In double dutch, a very long clothing line is folded in half, twisted for a braided effect (to thicken and hold it together), then looped again. One turner has the two ends and the other turner has the loop behind her waist. One hand turns clockwise; the other hand turns the rope counter-clock-wise. CeCe's counting establishes a rhythm as each woman takes her turn. A chorus of voices, led by the children, counts the number of successful jumps. A look of accomplishment transforms faces when they "get it," and everyone cheers others on, patiently allowing them to try as many times as they wish. Sarah's face shines with joy. Jessie euphorically punches the air with her fists. Eventually everyone "masters" double dutch, getting at least two successful jumps in, and all are ready to go again.

I lack coordination (numerous school gym teachers have confirmed this over the years) so it takes some coaxing before I finally take a turn at jumping. The women whoop and laugh when I shake my hips. I cannot jump the second rope. They encourage me to try again. To my utter surprise, on the second attempt I succeed. I shout—and a chorus of voices cheers with me.

Double dutch becomes for me a metaphor of "readiness" to change, and capacity for change, for both the group and the individual. While an organization can create a setting for community and change, readiness to change individual behavior is an individual choice.

After evening devotions, Africa talks about the role of psychology in substance abuse programs. "I don't think the key has to do with psychology and behavior modification and all of that book knowledge. It is us coming together learning from each other. I'm gonna do anything I have to do not to go back to being the same person I was. It don't take book knowledge as much as it just takes compassion. And since this is Christian-based, once you come into a relationship with God it's just something that you have to do in your spirit. It's not as easy as book knowledge because my flesh and my soul are always fighting against each other. It's a warfare: It's just about doing the right thing today, everyday, to me.

"This is my community, and I want to stay here and welcome the next sister who comes in. I want to work with her and make her part of the community. That's my vision, to just see through their faults and see through my issues with them and just to bring them into this community as a whole. So they can be a part of the community and add on to the next sister. That will keep building up the community. That's why I chose to stay here. To save another life. I'm here to help build up the community through loving my sister and letting her know that this can be your home. Just open up your heart and allow God to work. Through his love you'll be able to give love to the next sister. I'm grateful that God has delivered me from myself and loved me. It was only through his grace and his mercy that I'm here. That I survived fifteen years of crack addiction and abuse. I've had guns to my neck, knives. I'm grateful, and I'm going to do whatever it takes to bring that other person in."

After I turn off the recorder, Africa asks me, "What's your story, Michele?" She is the only person at Dover to ask me that question. I tell her about meeting the homeless man in Washington, D.C.

I also tell her about another encounter with a homeless man in a troubled ghetto of Cincinnati known as over the Rhine. My husband and I are there at the invitation of the Salvation Army to help them plan and host a neighborhood festival. During the festival's lunch, a man sat next to me at a picnic table. I admit to Africa how repulsed I was by this man. He limped, was hunched over, trollish, and possibly retarded. His skin was so disfigured, as if burnt, that I could not guess his race or age. He had no teeth and gummed his burger. He squinted at me through rheumy eyes. His body odor was so overpowering, I could barely keep from retching. Unlike another man and the two children who had also sat at this table and ignored me, he greeted

me and asked my name, introducing himself as Enu. When he asked
if second portions would be served, I said No, and offered him my
cookies. He smiled with simple delight and patted my knee. We ate in
silence. After I finished my burger, I stood and said goodbye. My back
was turned to him when Enu spoke. "Goodbye Michele." I turned,
surprised (no one else had remembered my name) and he said, "I love
you, Michele." Then he disappeared into the crowd. At that moment
I knew him, the way you recognize a celebrity, or a friend you have
not seen for years. I realized he was Jesus.

I am moved to tears as I tell her the story because I know she lived
the homeless life, and because, through her, I experience afresh the awe
of what happened. She is crying too. "Wow," she says. "Wow."

FIFTEEN
SPANNING BARRIERS

Tuesday, April 16, 2002

I wake up tired but calm—free of yesterday's emotional fullness—as if I have already said goodbye. At breakfast I hear someone say, "It's going to be warm." Tyrone, who is about nine, replies, "Eighty. That's high. High is warm. Low is cool."

I go to the guest bathroom near the library to blowdry my hair since it is before the 7:30 wakeup time. I see the children assembling in the cafeteria to catch their school bus. Frances's daughters wear bright plaid outfits and heart-shaped sunglasses. The women on cleanup and bus duty joke with them, enjoying the girls' high spirits.

The 8:00 a.m. Motherhood class meets in the chapel. The students have a test, which they take to the steady hum of the wall-mounted circulating fans. Class begins with a discussion regarding mistakes women made as mothers or siblings. Marcia strides from one side of the chapel to the other, a formidable, energetic woman with a powerful voice, shoulder-length, dark braided hair, a piercing glance, and a gold front tooth that glints when she smiles.

"Unconditional love is the ideal. Bonding starts in the womb. I understand this truth even though I am not a mother. I was pregnant once. Only once. I had an abortion. I thank God for forgiveness. I have a maternal feeling toward all the children. I have seen so many of 'my children' arrive and leave this place."

A new resident, Ashley, says something about her foster mother. Marcia pauses before taking up this new subject, guilt. "When are you going to talk out and heal the anger? You say you can't discipline because of the guilt. Sometimes our anger with children is justified, and we need to be just in our disciplining. Children need consistent discipline, not merciless spanking. Take into consideration the personality types of children, the circumstances, and your own emotional state. Address the trust issue: Ask, 'How can I show these children they won't have to worry again, whether it's about mom leaving or abuse?' God heals all wounds. Some things only God can do. In those times we have to relax, not become discombobulated." She illustrates with a few hypothetical examples, modeling what the mom says, and what the child says. "Remember, they look for love, safety, and security."

Next is Mary's class, called "Your Emotional and Spiritual Power" (based on a book by Dr. Richard Dobbins). Mary is about five feet tall, round, and gentle. She says, "I spent one year homeless and as a prostitute. I entered New Life with a broken leg after a guy drove over me in a truck. I had stolen some of his dope—there was a death threat out on me, too. I thought I would try to play this program, the way I played others. But when I entered the door, *Woosh*,"—she takes a deep breath—"God, the love of God, it was breathtaking. I couldn't stop crying. It was miraculous. I experienced no withdrawal from drugs at all. But I had severe withdrawal from addiction to the abuse. Fantasies, physical cravings. In the streets I would make men beat me. One guy, not a violent guy at all, I drove him to hit me. I remember once he said to me, 'Why do you do this to yourself?'"

Mary runs her fingers through her silver hair, and announces that there will be a quiz on the memory verse, Hebrews 11:1–3. Students write the passage from memory and hand it in. Lupita reads a character study paper about Noah for the class assignment. Mary continues a list from a previous lesson: "Healthy faith expresses anger constructively. Hurt people hurt other people. Avoid blowing up, or clamming up. Be aware of nonverbal cues. What are some constructive ways we can direct our anger?" Students answer: with writing, praying, singing, cleaning, exercising.

"Healthy faith balances work and play. It loves and forgives others, but we need to forgive ourselves first."

Anticipating alumnae and graduation weekend, Mary urges her students to "be sponges" spiritually and intellectually. She turns to the subject of depression, using her own battle with depression to illustrate. She weaned herself from medication when she first came to NLFG as a resident. "Depression can be a form of self-hatred. We don't feel comfortable in our own skin. Depression does not have to be a part of our lives; we choose to be in it." Mary closes the book and continues. "I was from an upper-middle-class background. My parents were well-to-do, they substituted material things for love—we had every material thing we needed. My father, when he was sober, would sometimes surprise us with a spontaneous trip, a nice vacation somewhere. But when he was drunk, oh boy. Look out. He was abusive." Lupita remarks that she can identify, saying, "Christ is our medicine."

Mary further defines depression. "It's emotional pain, sometimes also physical. Sadness, ranging from mild discouragement to despair. Loss of hope. There is a lowness of spirit. In your mind's eye, imagine your spirit when depressed: It's being squelched. Before we had hopelessness. Now we have hope."

Gisetta offers, "I felt numb."

Holly asks, "Can depression be hereditary?"

Mary nods, "Yes, it can be. My family and I were always labeled bipolar. But I'm not taking meds today. In my case that label was a trick of the enemy. And it can have a snowball effect: If we are performance-oriented, if we think we have to be perfect little moms or career women, then we only see the negative. Our unhealthy emotions led to our addictions. Every time I teach this class I get such healing." She mentions examples of depressed people found in the Bible such as Job, Elijah, Jonah; their symptoms were similar to ours: appetite loss or gain, sleep disturbances.

After the break, Mary picks up the subject of sex as addictive behavior. "Sometimes sex, even sexual abuse, is the addictive behavior. One risk, after graduation, is the need to 'have a man.'"

Sarah jokes that men are second-class citizens in her family, a household of women. She gets a laugh when she adds, "My dad would say, 'PMS means pack my suitcase.'"

As the class ends, the conversation shifts to bulimia and anorexia. Mary says, "It's cyclical. We will have a lot of women who struggle with it, then not so many. Now we are on the increase again. God will show you areas that need to be healed. Sometimes the wound will get larger, but the end process is complete healing." Mary points out the difference between remorse—regret over getting busted—and repentance—turning away from that thing. She quotes Romans 12:1–2 from memory, then paraphrases: "By this renewing of mind, we are transformed into the good, perfect, and acceptable will of God. We must allow the spirit of the Lord to become the dominating force in our lives."

At lunch, Liza and I perfect our imitation of gestures and malapropisms associated with different residents. For example she is known for pointing and screaming, "Aaaaaaghhh!" And we both appreciate Rosa's trademark "Oh my gooseness." Liza also claims to have "originated" the beauty queen wave, but I remind her that royalty, Queen Elizabeth for one, have been doing that wave for years.

Alumnae reunion and graduation weekend will take place in just a few days. It has been a long journey for those who will be graduating. But graduation weekend is not what occupies my mind as the sun sets and I finally drive home. Instead, I am thinking about seeing Rosa and Tawanda just as I leave. They are calling to me from the open window of the chapel where they are cleaning. It's a sunny day and they are in silly moods. Rosa mock-complains that "Tawanda is in here talking to herself." Tawanda retorts, "Hey, I ain't talkin' to myself. I'm talking to God!" Rosa says, "Hey, Michele, remember in Westminster when I told you that you remind me of someone, like a movie character, but I couldn't think of who? I got it now. I know who you remind me of. That girl who went down the rabbit hole, Alice. Alice in Wonderland."

PART THREE

OMEGA GROUP AND ALUMNAE

"You seem very clever at explaining words, Sir," said Alice.

"Would you kindly tell me the meaning of the poem 'Jabber-wocky'?"

"Let's hear it," said Humpty Dumpty. "I can explain all the poems that ever were invented—and a good many that haven't been invented just yet."

—From *Through the Looking-Glass,* Chapter VI.

Behold, I send you out as sheep in the midst of wolves; so be wise as serpents and innocent as doves.

—Jesus instructing his disciples,
Matthew 10:16 (RSV)

SIXTEEN
ESCAPE FROM PRISON

Friday, May 3, 2002

*M*y New Life experience made me feel much like a latter-day Alice in Wonderland. So it came as no surprise when Rosa identified me with Alice. She probably had several meanings in mind. In fact, I do hear from her, and a group of other residents, about their perception of me, among other matters. When the Omega group convenes for seven weeks during the summer, I find out whether their perceptions match up with my own interpretations.

Alice is symbol of innocence. My innocence, and theirs. She is an emblem of childhood, of child lost and, for these women, regained. That is why the organization so strongly resists a name change. The community remains "New Life for Girls" even though the "girls" range in age from eighteen to sixty-four. For the women of New Life, life has begun anew, beginning with girlhood.

Even though Alice knows nothing of Wonderland when she first falls into it, every child who reads the story recognizes that she is not afraid. Alice steps through the mirror, drinks from the bottle, and explores the new world. She exercises her intellect without compromising her sensitivity, or, as Jesus put it, she has the capacity to remain as wise as a serpent, yet as innocent as a dove.

Likewise, my perceived innocence combines their sense of "you can't possibly know what we have been through" with their appreciation for my willingness to try to know. Just like the mirror Alice steps through, theories of community are not merely a mirror, but a new way of looking at the world that also alters the way we look at ourselves.

Alice is also a boundary spanner. She moves from the real world to Wonderland and back again, gaining the capacity to translate for *each setting, and paving the way for others to follow her and safely reach the realm of adulthood. Alice does not discount the value of her experience in this passage (although many adults do discount or marginalize children, and addicts know all about marginalization). Nor does Alice accept the values of either world at face value. She challenges the nonsense and questions the assumptions of everyone, from the anxious rabbit to the imperious queen to the know-it-all, thin-shelled Humpty Dumpty. She is a member of both worlds, yet as a boundary spanner she risks becoming isolated, a member of neither. Every alumna of NLFG also stands in this balance: Will they be accepted or rejected? Will the hurdles in their new lives be insurmountable? Will the familiarity of the old life prove too seductive?*

So, too, I was about to learn whether I was accepted as a member of the New Life community, or rejected as an outsider; and in the longer run, whether my learning from the New Life community would be accepted or ignored, valued or explained away by the larger world.

A number of New Life residents have been to prison. To understand their experience one must be able to envision prison life. Prisoners are beyond an observation window, watched and controlled by computer-automated surveillance and security lockdown systems. They wear orange jumpsuits, and they all look the same. Most avoid eye contact with outsiders. It is a world of gritty realism, a world where experienced prison administrators readily admit they've never rehabilitated a single person. The job of these administrators is not to change prisoners but to keep them locked up for the term of their sentence. Ironically, as evidenced by high recidivism those who serve out their terms are primed to commit another crime and be locked up again.

There is an experiential dividing wall between the prisoners and visitors to prisons even greater than the bulletproof glass and security systems. Visitors watch them, thinking, *I will never be you and you will never be me.* Outsiders cannot fathom

how a person would make a series of decisions so foolish as
to wind up incarcerated. They think of their hard-earned tax
dollars going to prisoners' food and healthcare, and they sense
that it will all be wasted when the prisoners return to the
streets and find new ways to put others at risk. If politicians,
wardens, and prisoners themselves are pessimistic about prisoners' futures, how can anyone think otherwise?

Anyone who meets Osage or Fred will no longer en-
tertain such hopelessness. Fred spent thirteen years in prison,
five in a state facility for robbery and eight in a federal peni-
tentiary. At one time he and his wife Osage had a legitimate
business so profitable that they lived a lifestyle of affluence in
New Mexico. Drug trafficking added still more wealth—and
risk. Osage remembers, "Fred was a very open user, and I was
a closet user. I tried to keep things together."

When Fred was arrested, the federal government seized all
of his assets, worth millions of dollars. Osage did not have to
do prison time, yet she was a prisoner of her habit. She spent
eighteen years addicted before she entered New Life in 1997.
Now Osage and Fred are full time staff at NLFG. They have
also been trained to provide Christian counseling for married
couples.

Osage had been living and working in Phoenix for more
than a year and returned to York, Pennsylvania to remarry
Fred. Those months were particularly difficult for her. In addition to the transition, her mother died. Osage attended to
her last days and the funeral in Oklahoma. It was the first
loss she had grieved without depending on drugs or alcohol.
She still mourns her father, who hung himself when she was
nineteen, but her grief is shot through with memories of his
violence toward her mother. When Osage was a preschooler,
her father kidnapped her and her siblings from their mother.
His income as a court reporter allowed them to have a nice
home, a swimming pool, and horses. Osage says that her re-

union with her mother in adulthood was painful but brought closure.

She and Fred live in a city apartment owned by New Life, which they are renovating to provide transitional housing for NLFG graduates. They occupy the first floor. Osage has decorated the living room in a country motif, and it is fragrant with scented candles. There are framed pictures of family members. She is a petite, full-figured woman with animated, smoky eyes and a bow mouth. Her exotic beauty bears witness to her Latina and Native American heritage. One of the photos is of Osage and her older sister as cheerleaders.

Osage talks about her childhood in Arizona with the older sister she idolized. Her sister was popular, an honors student, and the beginning driver of a new yellow Mustang. "One afternoon we decided to go for ice cream after cheerleading practice. The convertible stalled. My sister got out of the car to flag down help." Osage raises her hands to her face as if shielding her eyes from the memory of what happened next. "The car didn't even slow down. I saw my sister fly onto its hood. It carried her one-hundred feet or more before her body slid off, onto the street." Osage's father blamed himself. Her mother blamed Osage. For Osage, it was one more reason to hate herself and reject God.

Osage became pregnant at sixteen and married the father. She named the baby after the sister she lost. Her first marriage lasted three years. By the time she was twenty-three, she had two failed marriages, three children, and an addiction to prescription diet pills. She married Fred over the telephone, while he was still in state prison. "I thought I could change him, and I thought if I picked from the bottom he would never leave me." After he got out of prison they were together for ten years before drug trafficking sent him back to prison. Counselors and psychologists told Osage her traumas were such that she would never lead a normal life. By this time, she was drinking heavily and desperate for income. An employment agent befriended her and invited her to church. Women from the church cared for her after a suicide attempt and told her about New Life.

Her view is that New Life has an impressive history, as a program with a track record of more than thirty years and with a base of many alumnae who have remained drug free for years. Still she knows people judge her for her past. "If there are problems at work, who do you think is the first person suspected?" In most employment situations, she would not be able to discuss her past, but New Life's track record helps graduates gain credibility in the church and in the workplace.

Osage misses aspects of her previous job. As administrative assistant to the CEO of a denomination, she planned major events and was pleased with her role in creating and coordinating a new program for single persons in ministry. She traveled and attended conferences, enjoying her independence. But she could no longer deny a calling to return to work for NLFG. During her first stint on the New Life staff, she helped found the New Mexico introduction program. She says her time away has helped her appreciate that experience. "I'm calmer with the women, not as controlling." Upon return, she started part-time as a teacher and counselor. Osage feels students open up to her because she is not in a position to discipline.

She talks about the emotional difficulty of reuniting with her husband after all that transpired. She loves him but must become reacquainted with the new Fred, as both of them have changed. Osage has two sons, a daughter, and one grandchild. She likes to show pictures of her family, including her great grandmother, who raised Osage's mother. Her great grandmother's husband was in the Spanish mafia, she remarks. Osage did not believe it until an aunt corroborated the story.

Fred is now a generous and grateful man, Osage says, and he weeps every time he attempts to describe what God has done for him. Their story is Kenda's in the making, an escape from the hopeless cycle of prison and reincarceration. Kenda's story emerges during a meeting of the Omega group.

The Omega group members are at the midpoint of their NLFG experience, having spent about three months at an introduction center, three months in the Alpha phase of their Dover residency, and now three months in the Omega phase. Ahead of them is one month in Emmanuel, during which they pray about what to do next: go to school, go to work, go home, or stay and work at NLFG. They begin transitioning into their decision during the last phase, R&O, which lasts about three to six months.

There are eight women currently in the Omega phase. Seven of them have agreed to participate in weekly group discussions with me over a 7-week period. In doing so, they are giving up an hour of their free time each week. There is no incentive to participate in terms of their progress or standing in NLFG, but as their discussion reveals, they view this as an additional class and value the opportunity to learn.

The first meeting with the Omega group is on May 3rd in the library. I tell the women that it is an opportunity to reflect. There are no requirements, and "street talk" is allowed. I ask the group to reflect on their lives before New Life and after, and how they experienced emotion as part of the healing process.

Holly speaks first. "I don't tell my emotions now, I show them. Before I came to NLFG I never showed them. Here I've been more emotional. I like to write my feelings down on paper because it helps me to look and see where I'm at, see where I've been and where I'm going."

Gisetta says, "I think it was a move of the Holy Spirit. I didn't sugarcoat it." She wipes tears from her eyes. "It really moved me, because so much has changed since then. At the time, prior to coming here, I didn't have my sons. They were already in the boys' home. So much has happened to them, to me. I've done a lot of healing but still have a lot more to do. God's working on it; I'm allowing him to. From the darkness to the light. That's what I see. No more hiding, no more fear. I'm so glad I'm out of it.

"I had myself so emotionally secluded because of the fear while I was using drugs, I couldn't even figure out why I was using them. I thought I used them as an excuse for the way I grew up. But it just made me feel worse, just enhanced these negative emotions I had. Back then I was ignorant, and I didn't know Jesus. That's what I'm trying to explain to my boys now. No secular program can ever change you, because they try to just focus on the drugs, not what was in here," she points to her chest, "all the junk inside of me. My boys, they don't realize that yet."

Lupita leans forward. "I needed to get it out to remind me where I did come from. Matter of fact, my last hit was Mother's Day last year. Thinking about it brings back memories. If I did not make this mistake, I would not have found God. I know I went through tough times, but there was a purpose for me to go through this; it brought me closer to him. Many programs out there are not of Christ and don't really work. I am so glad Christ picked me up and brought me here. It was tough—but I thank him every day. If I can get educated more and more, maybe I can touch people's hearts."

Sarah observes, "I just remember the stress and the striving I would do, all this stuff I would go through—the people and the hassle, this drama of trying to get something and never getting any satisfaction. Ever. It made me realize that God does turn around the evil you were doing and turns it into good, because here I'm really striving and I don't have drama and stress at all, but I'm getting fulfilled, getting something out of it, and pressing on to something of substance. I'm not just grasping anymore. I am actually partaking of Christ.

"There was so much drama: 'So-and-so did this to so-and-so, we did this, they said this, we don't have your money, they got your money.'" Sarah shakes her head, her laugh is tinged with sadness. "The relationships people had, absolutely no trust anywhere. People lived recklessly, sinfully. Out of control. People didn't even know what day it was. I would stay up for so long I would lose track of what day it was. It got to the point where I didn't make any appointments or plans because I couldn't keep them. Finally you sleep for two to three days, and the world just passes you by."

Kenda is next. Her voice sounds so quiet, childlike, at first. She nervously drums the table with her fingers.

"Thinking about, uh prison … it bothered me, but it's also a blessing I'm here now. Before I came here I was in prison. I wasn't saved. Like Sarah says, there was drama, day in and day out. Dealing with the kooks and weirdos in there all day long, the lesbians and bull-dykes, cussing and fighting and just trying to make something out of the day while being there. Between the four walls every day, it's hard, especially when you want to be out—you want to beat the system, but you can't. You just want some meaning in your life. Fighting, cussing, talking on the phone, fighting someone about what we were going to watch on TV. It drove me crazy. I was on medication I had never been on in my life because I was depressed, and I couldn't sleep, so I was taking medicine to help me sleep. It was very, very hard.

She shifts in her chair. "A lot of times I try to forget about prison, but I know I'm not supposed to forget what I came from. It's hard to think that I put myself in that predicament. I never thought for a million years that I would be in jail. Never thought that I would do the things I did. Ever. But like someone said, if those things had not happened, I wouldn't have had a relationship with the Lord. I would probably have died and gone to hell.

"It got to the point where I thought I was going to spend the rest of my life in jail. And I just gave up. Which caused me to fall deeper and deeper into what I was into. I thought there was no hope, no one to help, and I was surrounded by the chaos, total chaos. I thought that I would never get out. Die there, or die in the streets. But God had other plans. Although it was a struggle and still is, I know he has his hand stretched out to me." Kenda begins to cry. "A lot of times I'm afraid to take it. I don't know why."

The room falls silent. Someone passes a box of tissues to Kenda. I suggest that one thing we can look for as researchers is whether there is a pattern, even in the "chaos, the drama." I challenge them to ask, "What am I seeing?"

Lupita comments, "It was a hard decision for a lot of us; we had to say goodbye to children, mothers, even people in heaven. We're walking with God, rather than being out there, in the alleys getting killed or stabbed. We feel good being here.

"My father died four years ago, and I know he's looking down on me. He used to call the house when I was high. I'm not going to kick myself anymore because God already got all my sins and threw them away, and the devil can't throw that at me. I'm not going to think about yesterday. I'm going to think about tomorrow. God gave us these bodies to enjoy, not to destroy. Therefore I'm glad God did find all of us."

I show the group a sketch of a tree with sturdy roots, trunk, branches and leaves, to serve as a visual metaphor for community. Communities are composed of behavioral systems, relational systems, value systems, and underlying assumptions, according to one theory, I explain, showing them the four descriptors written on adhesive-backed slips of paper.

"On what parts of the tree does each label belong?" I ask them.

Sarah: "Is the relational system trunk or leaves?"

Gisetta: "Underlying assumptions go with the roots."

Sarah: "Behavioral system goes on the leaves."

Several women suggest that the value system should label the trunk of the tree. By process of elimination, they attach the relational system to the branches. Underlying assumptions are often hidden, as most of the roots of a tree. The "disconnects" between espoused values (what we say) and behavior (what we do) suggest underlying assumptions that drive a community's culture. Conversely, if the espoused and underlying values align, there are no major behavioral "disconnects."

Next is a list of the six "metafunctions" of community, describing what community does: companionship, celebration, exchange, safety, significance, and sanctity (or a sense of the sacred). The question, Were these functions present in your life prior to New Life? sparks a lively discussion.

Sarah's laugh is hollow. "Maybe companionship. Gangs."

Kenda: "Exchange."

Sarah: "There was no safety, no significance, no celebrations. Definitely no sanctity."

Kenda: "We may have thought there was celebration, but it always turned into depression, disaster, or chaos."

Community connections were either missing or distorted.

Gisetta: "Everything was inside out. Every term you have there, we could find the total opposite. Instead of safety, we had fear, danger."

Holly: "*In*security. *In*significance."

Sarah: "Exchange was money and drugs."

"It was dangerous," Lupita says. "People wanted sex for drugs. They put guns to my head. I should have been dead many times. There were angels protecting me."

Gisetta: "Nothing was fair in drugs and war. Significance? There was none."

Lupita: "We had celebrations for Satan."

Sarah: "Or no celebrations."

"How does this relate to the prison experience some of you described, that stripping away of identity?" I probe.

Heads nod when Gisetta responds, "You're just a number."

Holly mentions her constant depression, "I was so behind on my bills. I was always in a sad state."

Sarah: "We were secluded. Especially from our families. Withdrawal from community … ." Her point is greeted with murmurs of agreement. "None of us had any true friends."

Gisetta: "It was a dog-eat-dog world."

Sarah and others describe a vicious cycle of promiscuity. "Adultery, sharing spouses, that was the lifestyle." Lupita adds, "Men threw women at each other like toys."

Gisetta: "It was hell."

Sarah: "Nothing pure and good. The opposite of sanctity."

"During the nights the demons came in me," Lupita says. "That's when I started my mess. I remember things coming into me, and I knew demons were in control."

Is this community, or something else? The women think for a moment. They coin their own phrase: *Anti*-community.

Kenda, who agreed to serve as timekeeper, lets everyone know the hour has ended. The women celebrate as a group and take comfort that these things are in the past. For the next week they must reflect on their first impressions of Dover.

As they gather their notebooks and prepare to leave, Sarah says, "Once you're here a while you realize you're not here for a drug or alcohol problem; you're really here because God called you."

After the Omega group meeting, Kenda settles into a plastic chair by the window in the Kindness Hall's lounge. She is another who dispels myths about life after prison. Her laugh is boisterous and infectiously mischievous. The afternoon light falls across her face, illuminating her world-weariness in spite of her youth. She sighs and says that she prefers one-on-one conversation to group interaction.

"I was convicted on nine counts of armed robbery and expected to serve a 20-year term. We were looking for money for drugs. I served nine months in prison before coming here."

There were power plays and manipulation in prison, everyone vying for respect, Kenda says. "People were intimidated by us. They weren't going to cross certain boundaries. They knew our backgrounds, and they knew what would happen to them if they did. I was a carnal Christian, so even though I got saved when I was in prison, I did everything that a Christian wasn't supposed to. Even physical violence.

"I got into fights two or three times, because somebody got smart with me or tried to hit on me. One of the women approached me and we got into a fight because I had already let her know, 'Don't come in my face with that,' and she did it anyway. I had to prove a point, you know what I'm saying, so it wouldn't happen with nobody else."

And Kenda won her fights.

"A lot of times the fight wouldn't go on very long because the officers would come and break us up and put us in lockdown, where you go into these individual cells by yourself; you're locked in this little cell maybe for ten days. When you get into the fight you have a hearing officer, and you sit and talk with her. They ask what happened, and ask if you're guilty or not—it's like a little hearing so you can get off lockdown to get back to your dorm."

Kenda's route from prison to New Life was fraught with obstacles. "First I went to court where I had the preliminary hearing and was indicted. The judge let me know what I was facing, and the state offered me a deal. I took the deal—four-to-nine years—because that was the lowest they were offering. My lawyer, she was a sweetheart. I was very mean and ugly to her, but she stuck with me. She was trying to find programs for me, you know. Public sector programs. The doors weren't opening at the secular programs. Then she looked into Teen Challenge in Maryland. The doors looked like they were about to open, but they shut in my face. I gave up hope and was about to take the four-to-nine years at the state penitentary. And then she found out about New Life for Girls. There was still a waiting process, and I was getting impatient. So I had to go through the process of getting all the information, sending the money in, my family having to get involved in that."

Though Kenda's face appears composed and cool, she drums her fingers on the table, faster and louder, anxiety surfacing.

"I never, *never* before asked my family for any money. But my sister was there for me; she was in court through the whole ordeal. My court date was after my NLFG bed date, so I had to get a new bed date. But God opened the doors for me, because I went to court August first and had a bed at New Life on August second. I got released from jail August first. It was amazing that the judge trusted me to let me out for those twenty-four hours to get to New Life because when I first went in front of him he told me I would never see the streets again.

"A friend of mine took me home for a day. I could have easily got high, or had a drink or smoked a cigarette. I wouldn't do any of it. I just went straight to the house and I stayed there. I got to New Life at seven the next morning." Kenda mulls over her readiness at that time.

"At first I was just happy to be out of jail. Although I almost didn't come here. But I knew that if I didn't come I would be on the run again. And I knew if I was on the run I would get sucked back into drugs." She presses her hands to her eyes, as if trying to blot out a memory. "I didn't want that. I had been through a lot when I was getting high. So I just made the decision to come"

Her first impression of New Life was that it would be different from anything she had experienced before. "This is the first time I went through a program, except I did an outpatient mental thing, one time. It was nothin' compared to this. When I got to Dover everyone was really nice to me, teaching me about God and Jesus. As time went on I had problems because I didn't want to deal with all the restrictions, and I always had trouble submitting to authority, so that was a big obstacle. They had some staff that were younger than me, and I thought they were picking on me. I was alone for so long, and was used to doing what I wanted to do; it was hard to submit to authority. It was really hard, regardless of what age the staffers were."

Kenda sighs and looks out the window. "Even now, I can't have contact with my fiancé. We've been together for ten years. He proposed in '98. Because we're not married we can't have contact. That was particularly hard for me to do, and it still is. I have some restrictions on me now because I tried to send a letter to him. I got caught and got in trouble for it. That happened in April. The spirit is willing and the flesh is weak." Her laugh is apologetic, vulnerable. "I haven't tried since. But my family, my younger sister especially, has a big problem with understanding why I can't have contact with him. I tell her it is because they believe, especially if you aren't married, that it may be a hindrance with your walk with God."

She pauses, then adds. "I feel differently about it, but that's just me. I know they won't let the ladies have contact with their boyfriends if they used drugs together or if there was abuse going on. I met my man when I was sixteen, and there was never any abuse. I watched my mother get beat up by my stepfather, and that's one thing that I refuse—to let a man beat me up. He never did drugs with me; when I was doing heroin he didn't know about it, and I wouldn't do it when I was home. I was like a functional addict. He never used, but he went to prison. That's when I started using crack cocaine. That's another thing—that he went to prison. I have a lot of difficulty dealing with that, and NLFG made me feel like he was a bad person because he went to prison, but what I went to prison for was far worse than what he did."

Kenda clarifies, "He was a dealer. He's home now. Did four years. But he never used drugs." She stops drumming her fingers and leans forward, a confident expert in these matters.

"From my experience, knowing the streets, a lot of times drug dealers won't start using because they know they won't profit, they'll become their own best customer. If they're using and they're trying to sell it's not gonna mix, because they're using their own product. They also see the result of people using. Anyway, that has a lot to do with why NLFG won't let me have contact with him—because of the lifestyle he used to live. It bothers me because they don't want to hear about how he's living now. He's working, back in college; he's not stupid. He's following all the rules that society would have him live by."

She says he is also a believer. "His mother is a Christian, and he grew up in a Christian home. Even though he was a dealer—sometimes kids grow up and go the other way. But he was saved. He got saved in prison just like I did. But he knows the Bible inside and out because he grew up in it."

Kenda admits she continues to keep up with him from time to time through her family. She chokes back tears as she continues. "It was really hard because we communicated from the time when we were in jail. Then in intro it just cut off, and I couldn't let him know why or what. He supported me coming here, but there's been no contact whatsoever. He must be wondering what's going on."

In intro, Kenda learned that she could get to know good people who didn't always have a hidden agenda. "In my past I was always dealing people who wanted something. There was always a lack of trust … ."

She draws a breath and the words stream out. "I had to learn how to trust all over again. Even though I was in the streets and I hung with certain people, I was lonely. We were all manipulators, and we were no good for each other unless we had something for each other. Or I would hang around people because I just wanted friends. I knew that a lot of them were just there because I had money or drugs. I had my family, but I didn't go to them because of the state that I was in. I didn't want them to know my dark side. I didn't see my family for two or three years. My parents are deceased. I have two grandmothers, some uncles, aunts, a stepgrandmother, father, and four sisters and a brother. I'm the oldest.

"My couselor at Westminster was Chere, but I was always talking to Dennis or Valerie. And just having them there was like a little nest. When I got to Dover it was overwhelming at first. I stayed to myself, didn't talk to anybody. Then after you get in the swing of things, you get used to it. There's a lot more freedom here, a lot more space."

"I have good friends here, and that's a good thing, because when I was in the streets I didn't have any friends. It was hard to trust anybody else. You're taking a chance here by making friends. During intro my friends were Jolane, Brooke, Tawanda, CeCe, Winona, and Holly. Here I added Martee, who moved a few days before I did, and Patti, who has been here for a while. We've gotten close. Bosom buddies."

The transition to Dover from Westminster was a struggle, Kenda says. "The day I graduated from intro, I cried. I hugged Dennis, and I didn't want to let him go. I told him 'I love you' and that I was grateful for the rebukes and disciplines that I got from him. At first I hated him." She cackles. "I *hated* him! I was getting in trouble so much, getting a discipline every day, but he gave it to me in love. And he would make me read Scriptures." She rolls with laughter: "I was so rebellious, so rebellious, but it worked out for the best, and I thank him every time I see him."

Kenda sighs again, leans back. "You know, when you're in intro, it's more like you're going to school. You have your little chapel services and go to choir meets. But when you're here you have more time to seek God, because the classes are so intense up here they blow you away. Intro is just like a starter kit to get you ready for the big place, the big house. The classes here teach you to deal with issues that get tucked in for so long, get rid of them, and leave them behind—to give them to God. And you get broken. If you allow God to work through you through the classes and prayer, you break here.

"It's really up to the person if they want to be broken. A lot of times people don't. They go straight through here and graduate. I've seen a lot of people just fly through the program and not get broken at all. Some people put on an act just to get through it. I don't understand why would they even bother. You're not here under a gun; it's voluntary. You can leave. A lot of people put on a show. I really don't want to know why they do it because that's between them and God. But I've been broken, and I still need to be broken in a lot of areas.

"I graduate on October 26. And then I'm going home!" She throws her head back, laughing gleefully. "I haven't been with my family for four years. I've seen them once since I've been here. I went home one time for a 12-hour visit in January. Didn't see them when I was in prison. Writing, calling, it's not the same."

The curtains billow in an afternoon breeze coming through the open window. She turns reflective again, considering her future. "I might go to college. But I don't know yet. I might go to a community college.

"I've changed a lot. I'm not as rebellious as I used to be. I know I'm not the same person I was a year ago. And I've learned that all you have to do is ask and believe that he will give it to you. Prayer works. I didn't used to think it worked, but even when I was in my mess I would pray and it seemed like God would answer me. Now when I look back, I would ask God to send someone to help me, and he would do it and I would turn them away."

She shakes her head. "I think, 'You fool, you're so stupid.' I believe that I wanted to stop, but I didn't know a way out. Then I went to prison, and it gave me some relief. When I found out how much time I was facing, I got scared because I didn't want to be in prison for the rest of my life. Then God opened the door for me to come to New Life.

"I never used to cry. My heart was stone. I didn't care about anybody, because I didn't care about myself. At Westminster I cried some, but I didn't get broken until I came here. I wanted to run when I was in Westminster. I wanted to leave so many times. But they wouldn't let me. I also thought about leaving Dover, but in my heart I knew I wanted to stay. God had begun to deal with me. At Westminster, I wanted to run because I was familiar with running. My whole life was running."

Osage and Fred's escape from prison represents a future that Kenda sees for herself. Months later, as I begin to talk to alumnae of New Life, I meet a woman whose story resembles Kenda's in a different way. Also African American, Mae, 41, has remained free of drugs and alcohol since her graduation from New Life in 1987. She describes her current career as an administrator and counselor, overseeing a juvenile detention program in the New England state where she lives with her husband and children.

"I landed this job in 1990, a year after leaving the NLFG staff. This profession has a high burnout rate, but I love it. My concern for the children overrides everything else. I have such a concern to see them make it in life. Things they're born right into, their homes, things they are exposed to, it's sad and if I can make a difference, that's my goal, to make a difference in their lives. I do pray with them sometimes. I know what they say about separation of church and state and all that, but no one has ever said anything to me about it, the Lord put it on my heart to start doing it about two years ago, as a matter of fact both the staff and the youth tell me they like me doing that."

Her no-nonsense delivery reminds me of Kenda. And her voice softens, in that sudden way Kenda's can soften, when I ask her about her favorite class at New Life.

"It was called 'Growing up Spiritually.' Just knowing that was my life, from being bound by drugs and the things of the world, and that I had been freed, and I never knew that type of freedom before, never. I never knew I could be free like that."

SEVENTEEN
RE-EDUCATION OF A RACIST

Friday, May 17, 2002

The Omega group participants in attendance today reveal the types of communities to which they belonged prior to NLFG. Their descriptions are bracketed with laughing, as if they are retelling an inside joke.

Tawanda says, "We were a group of users, and our interest was in using together. There were unofficial leaders. We were from the same neighborhood. I was the youngest, but I was tall for my age."

"I was in with a group of people who all used the same kind of drug," says Sarah. "We all lived in the same town. The leader, the one that people listened to, has the most drugs, money. Naturally, being an addict, you want to be around the drugs and money. I fit in really well. Another girl and I hung out together, and we pretty much had the whole town. We were the main people I guess you could say. But there were so many people wanting to talk to you all the time, there was no peace. Someone was always asking, 'Can you give me a front (an advance on drugs)?' When you're not dealing the big big drugs where you can be in back, but dealing for the big drug dealer, you're usually high yourself, and thinking the cops are after you all the time. Even when you try to rest and find a place where nobody will know, they find you." There is sadness in her laugh. "No safety."

Brooke reveals, "My group was my family; they introduced me to drugs. When I first started using I would go to them, because I didn't know anybody. Even my family members would rip me off, because I was green—didn't know the tricks of the trade. They take advantage of you. I started using more and more. I had the money because I worked, and they knew I was the kind of person who would spend my money and give them more than I was going to use. I started getting smart, I got to know people so I could go straight to them, then to the drug dealer.

"I would run for people, sell for them. They would keep me in their house, and I would stay a few days and smoke and smoke, because I made so much money for them. I did whatever I needed to do to get high. I even got to a point when I lost my self-respect. I was using my body to get the drugs, and I didn't care."

Tawanda agrees that relationships were risky and superficial at best. "They build your trust up, and then all of a sudden, at the first indication of trouble, forget it. For example, if I woke up sick they would flicker. Suddenly your 'friends' are not there for you. If they have extra, fine, but if not you suffer."

Racism comes up for the first time since I began my visits to NLFG. I give the women handouts I created that illustrate the way they came together voluntarily as groups on three different occasions: Two illustrations are of different meetings of the same class, and the third is a larger group illustration labeled "Rec Time." The latter illustration probably helped to reveal views on racism, since the key identified whether the group seated at each game table was Latin American, African American, European American, or mixed.

Then I ask if they see any patterns.

There is tension in the room and little eye contact. Groupings they observe are "positive" people (versus "negative"), how far people have progressed in their spiritual maturity, or how far along in the NLFG program residents are. Another factor is level of competition for games. Racism is not explicitly mentioned as a defining factor.

Most of the women say they generally play the same games with the same group. Gisetta: "I choose not to play spades because I don't like the competition involved. That doesn't mean every group is competitive like that. I just choose not to play it. It's a lot of pressure to be that competitive, and I don't want to be in that environment. That's just my view. I'm not saying anything against anyone. But sometimes attitudes aren't good."

Mealtime seating is another story. Tawanda says, "Our little community, we sit at the tables. Or when we study I would sit at the round table, everybody around me." She laughs, spreading her arms in royal fashion. "Stretch my stuff out. Booths you can't do that. But I like everybody around me, I like being the center of attention all the time."

Gisetta adds, "I like to sit where I can see the entire room, even when I eat."

"Right, I don't like to sit in a booth with my back to everybody, facing the wall. I don't like that at all," Sarah agrees.

"I like to sit with people who are positive, not negative." Lupita says. "I stay away from certain crowds; I know we all have issues, and it's better for me to stay away."

"Birds of a feather flock together," says Gisetta.

"Not true," retorts Tawanda.

Lupita agrees with Gisetta. She has to make herself heard over a clamor of voices. "If you're all acting the same way or think the same way, you're going to hang around together. There are some that think alike. Some like to be alone, and some like to be in groups."

Brooke says, "It depends on your maturity level and Christian walk. People who come in from intro, and people in Omega aren't going to be on the same level—know what I mean? There's one person who says 'Man, you don't talk to me anymore.' It bugs me. It's not that I'm better than her, it's just where I am and she is. We're at two different levels. I'm learning a balance because I'm not that strong to rise to that level yet. I don't know what to say, where to go. It's hard being at this place because you don't want to feel like you're better, that you know more, because we come from the same place. But not everybody understands that yet. The classes make you grow each month. A lot."

"It's not just the classes that make you grow," says Sarah, "it's the situations you're in, the things you go through with different people, the problems you run into, and how you respond. It's hard to be humble. That's one thing you definitely learn here: how to be humble."

During the group discussion Kenda and Tawanda grow quiet. After this session, Kenda will skip meetings until the last two.

The group adjourns. As she helps tidy the room, Tawanda comments that she will help in any way but will not talk in the group discussions. She seems agitated and tells Marilyn she will be right up for choir. When everyone else leaves the room she says that she is upset by some of the opinions expressed. She points to different seats in the room where women were sitting and bursts out, "She's holier than thou, she's arrogant, and she's racist." Even though names were not mentioned during discussion, she seems to know who was in the suggested "out" group. It is she, Patti, and Kenda, all African-American women. Tawanda insists that it is race that sets them as outsiders relative to the other women and resents the implication that they are spiritually immature.

I make a mental note that Tawanda arrived late. She did not greet me with her usual smile when I first saw her as I drove up, so she may have other issues that she is dealing with today. Still, the tension in the room was palpable. I am glad Tawanda is able to express her feelings to me, and I tell her so.

Two weeks later, during a fundraising banquet for New Life, Tawanda grabs my hand and won't let go. "Please forgive me," she whispers. "Forgive you for what?" I ask. "I said things to you after that class I should not have said." I reply, "You did not say anything wrong. I'm glad you are able to tell me how you feel." "No," she insists, "what I said to you was wrong. I won't let go of your hand until I know you've forgiven me." Tawanda, usually so cheerful, looks stricken. I repeat, "I don't see the need. In my opinion, you have said nothing that requires forgiveness. But if it will make you feel better, fine." Tawanda looks relieved. "Thank you, Michele."

Later conversations with staff and alumnae help clarify what the residents are feeling and experiencing. Ursula, a recent graduate and NLFG staff member who lives off campus, experiences racism living in a rural part of the larger community—but not at NLFG. When she thinks of her current geographic community what comes to mind, Ursula says, is racism. "I guess because I'm the only black person out there. Everyone is not like they are at New Life. It's the real world. There's a lot of racist people out there. The way they talk to me, the way they look at me. I know the looks, I know what it is. It doesn't bother me, but I see it 'cause it's for real. This is the first time I've ever experienced that because I'm from Detroit—there are a lot of African Americans there. Other than that, it's real nice." She chuckles, and adds, "They aren't burning crosses in my yard or nothing, and not everybody is like that. I can't say what community was like in Detroit, because I was always high. I wasn't getting involved in anything."

Another alumna, Reba, admits her own racism, describing how she changed at New Life. Reba is forty-two, single, and lives alone in her own home in a city in Ohio. She leads a busy life, working full time in the finance department of a manufacturing firm. She runs a candle-making business on the side with relatives and stays active in her church and with other volunteer activities. She leads a women's Bible study that meets weekly. After living as an addict for fourteen years prior to New Life, Reba delights in reporting that she has been drug and alcohol free ever since her graduation in 1988.

Originally from a small town in Arizona, Reba thinks of NLFG as a "learning place," where the first step for her was to learn how to appreciate individuals from different cultures, culminating with an encounter with a "sandpaper sister": "I grew up in a little town. I wasn't used to being around different cultures. What I mean by that is I had the choice to be around certain people if I wanted to. At NLFG you don't have that choice. You're all there together. It was interesting in the beginning. You're there with blacks and Hispanics, and there's different food, everything. It was just different than what I was used to. Before being born again, you think in a stereotyped way or you are prejudiced. The Lord really did work in my heart and I began looking at people not as a threat but as a brother or sister. But it was a learning process; it didn't happen overnight. Definitely a culture shock." She laughs, remembering.

"There was a particular girl there that I just could not get along with, and it was not because she was Hispanic. She was from Brooklyn, and I'm from Arizona. We just clashed for several months. It came down to one chapel service where the speaker really hit home on things like unity and forgiveness and getting along. After the service we saw each other and said, 'We have to talk.' We made a time and sat in the chapel. We talked things out, and became good friends after that. And we were not a threat to each other any more."

In fact, Reba, the "small town girl," had an opportunity to apply what she learned when she served as the Bronx intro center director shortly after her graduation. Reba still feels drawn to the inner city where her church is located and where, in an evening mentoring program, she helps teens who face difficulties similar to those she encountered in her own youth.

EIGHTEEN
THE WOMAN WHO FOUND HER BRAIN

Friday, May 31, 2002

*T*o begin this week's session we review *differenct* ways we can ob- *serve: look for patterns, changes, groupings, and "disconnects" be- tween what community says and does. I ask them, using their written reflection assignment from last week, to compare their intro center and Dover first impressions. Is there anything else we might observe?*

Gisetta underscores the importance of structure and consis- tency: "When I was out in the world, in my mess, I didn't have structure or routine in my life—no kind of consistency. Here there's a whole structure. Routine. A time and place for everything." On connecting with people, she observes, "There were positives and negatives. We worked together. We had jobs, teamwork, organization. But sometimes there was a lack of teamwork, anger, or frustration. In fact, that's how I learned how to respond to people, and that's where I learned I was changing also. When I had to deal with people, which I didn't really want to do out in the world. I was more to my- self then; it was just me and my sons. Where I used to react out of anger I was learning how to respond. It was through Christ in me that I was able to do that. Otherwise it would have been different. When I would get thoughts that I wasn't changing, I knew that was a lie. It helped me communicate with other people. Through other people I learned who I was. I also knew who I wanted to be around, who I did not want to be around, and who I couldn't be around. God would use people to bring things forth that were in me. Often what I saw as negative was where I needed to change.

"How we respond also has to do with the background we came from," Holly suggests. "Some come from abuse, from Christian families, from no families, but everyone had the same common thing: They were all messed up on something. But we all found the same thing, Jesus, and he healed us."

I ask if there is a common denominator in the family backgrounds of residents.

"Yes." Gisetta says. "But that doesn't always mean drugs or alcohol. Could be depression, low self-esteem, rejection, negativity. And it doesn't always have to lead to drugs."

Holly disagrees. "My family was never dysfunctional, but my friends' families were and I think a little bit rubbed off on me."

Lupita recalls a lack of affection and love in her family that gave her low self-esteem. "Growing up, my parents were so jealous of each other. I became very jealous. Now that I know Christ I don't have to be insecure like that. It is a lack of education in the family, also. I had a friend with parents who were a good couple, went to church. My friend died two years ago: She was shot in the head and left to die. My point is that she grew up bad although her parents were Christians. They seemed like the perfect family. I don't understand that part."

The community responds to new people coming in by opening its arms wide, according to the women.

Lupita wiggles in her chair, eager to chime in. "It feels good when someone new comes in because there is another girl who will get saved. When I came in it was like God said, 'You'll be okay here; you're in a good home. You won't get beat up.' In the streets, every day I was getting beat up. It's been a year since I've had my hair pulled or my teeth knocked out. Here nobody hits me. What more can I ask? Small groups, big groups, it doesn't matter, as long as your sisters are with you. I feel a peace I have never felt before."

Gisetta explains, "At the introduction center I was in, the staff was freshly graduated, and I think they still had issues that had not been dealt with—it was obvious. A lot of things went on that were so extreme. When I came here, it was a breeze. I almost didn't come, but now I'm glad I did." She emphasizes that group discussion is important, adding, "It's good because you bring things into the light, as much as it hurts. Before I was hiding so much. The more we talk about it, the more we heal."

The group decides to construct a chart that illustrates resident turnover at the introduction centers represented in the room, in terms of the percentage who "graduate" to Dover. Since the resident population changes continually, they make their own group's residency period the time frame.

As the chart is completed they make an interesting discovery: Turnover among residents in their intro centers ranged from 42–60 percent. However, among those who made it to Dover, only two residents have left, less than 5 percent of the adult resident population.

This discussion of group healing comes up again weeks later during a conversation I have with Samanda, a 1995 graduate of New Life. She says that when these women discuss healing, they mean far more than just the physical.

Samanda lives on a tidy street of townhomes, not far from the college she attends. She is a 49-year-old African American woman with a broad smile whose energy and enthusiasm bely her age. Samanda says she is the proud mother of two adult sons and four "wonderful" grandsons. This is her eighth year of being drug-free, she says, and her health is good even if her waistline is broad. She laughs ruefully. "When I went into

NLFG, I was a perfect size eight. Now I'm a sixteen, which I'm not too pleased with, but it's okay. Right now I'm in an aerobic dance class. And I walk a lot. So far so good."

Her infectious laughter weaves through the conversation. She shares a comfortably furnished two-story townhome with her elderly mother. A sense of orderliness and peace pervades their home, a striking contrast to the journey these two women made to reach this point in their relationship.

Samanda was a functional addict, who worked full time as she kept her habit fed and hidden. In spite of a profound learning disability and barely graduating from high school, she managed to land a well paying clerical job with an insurance company, keeping it for eleven years. In fact, her drug use did not begin until after she left that job.

She provides a glass of iced tea for her guest and slips into a chair at her dining room table. "I enjoyed my job until I couldn't do it anymore. I worked with claims benefits. I had to code so many a day and process so many a day to meet a quota every month. If I didn't meet that quota it would affect my rates. I was getting frustrated because I got to the point where I was bringing work home. Back then, I had to process 250–300 claims a day. That was a lot for one person. If you process so much you wind up making mistakes. They would catch my mistakes, up to a certain point, and give me a warning. It was just a lot. The job was good, the money was good, but it was a frustrating job. Too much competition. And I am the type that if you train me to do one thing and four or five months later you change it, it's hard for me. And that would hold up the department's productivity. If you couldn't keep up, you were out. They gave me an ultimatum. They were going to demote me but not cut my pay. I felt degraded. It took me six-and-a-half years to get where I was. Eventually they fired my boss, my supervisor, and my manager; they got rid of the whole department.

"After that, I worked with pension for the clergy at a de-nomination's headquarters. I worked there for a good while. That's where I started doing drugs. I guess if I really wanted to go back there I could. They tried to help me through my addiction by sending me to an outpatient therapy program. A secular program. They put a lot of money out for me. It was not working, the secular program. I just didn't trust to open myself up to the counselors. I still repressed a lot. I just didn't want them to know my situation.

"My dad wasn't there for me. A lot of my bitterness and anger came from my father because I wanted to communicate with my Dad and he wasn't there. Then I started hiding behind drugs. I did that for three-and-a-half years, and I was getting tired. God had begun moving people out of my life, people I loved, because I truly believe he did not want me to die like that. So he started taking people out of my life, like my aunt, my mom's baby sister. She was like my sister. We hung together, did a lot of things together. Matter of fact, she was the one who turned me on to drugs," Samanda sighs. "And she died. God came to me in a dream, told me he was going to take her. I didn't want that to happen, but he had his reasons.

"She had cancer. Nobody knew. She was only forty-six, but they say she had the heart of an eighty-year-old woman because of the drugs. After she died, I didn't have a reason to be high. I couldn't continue to do drugs after she died. My children kept telling me, 'Mom, we don't want you to die like that.' I told them, 'I'm not going to.' But in my head I had a picture of myself dying. That's when I cried out for help. I just got to the point where I needed to get some help and fast. I heard of Teen Challenge, but they wouldn't take me because I was too old. I was thirty-eight.

"They told me it was for teenagers, and then they gave me the number for NLFG. The young lady who was there

heard the anger and frustration in my voice. She said, 'Samanda, don't worry. We're going to pray. We're going to get
you a bed.' And I'll never forget her. She stayed on the phone
with me, prayed with me." Samanda shakes her head, chuckling. "They told me, 'You can come.' I'm thinking, 'I'm going
to do three months.' But I did fifteen months in the program.
I went in the Westminster intro center first, for four months. I
told them I wasn't going to stay. I was going to get cleaned up,
because I had children, and then I wanted to go back home. I
went from there up to Dover. Deep down inside I wanted to
go home, but I didn't want to go home because I knew God
was not finished with me yet. He wanted to do a little operation on me, show me some things. And he did."

Samanda pauses, folding her hands on the spotless tabletop before continuing. "I'm glad I stayed. My mom had my
boys and they were fine, so that was a time for me. I was a
young mom. I had my first son when I was seventeen and my
second when I was twenty-five, but I was always a single parent. I had to do everything; I had to take care of the kids and
work, and when things went wrong I had to run to school,
or to the hospital. I mean there was a lot of things on me. I
just wanted a way out; I was just tired, and I got to the point
where my back was to the wall. That was my freedom, being
at NLFG, and I enjoyed it. I loved traveling with them, going out witnessing, reaching young girls, just being a part of
it. They really helped me out a lot, showed me a lot, taught
me a lot."

Samanda clarifies, "When I say tired, I think it was mental,
not so much physical. In my mind, I wanted to go on, and
then I didn't want to. I really thought I had it together. After
three months, I was good, I was dried out, I was fine, and I
could go back and get me a job, go on with my life. It was
at that point I found out I wasn't really dealing with myself.
I wasn't dealing with the issues I needed to be dealing with:
my emotions, my feelings about men, my children. I knew I

wasn't being truly honest with myself as far as what I really, really wanted to do. So I just stayed. I think if I had left I'd be right back out there again. But being there for those fifteen months turned my life completely around."

Samanda shares a story that dramatically illustrates how stereotypes can jeopardize a person's recovery. "I was diagnosed as having a learning disability, I'm dyslexic. I talk whatever, however. Sometimes I put the verb before, they don't always come out the right way. I started my first college classes while at NLFG. New Life and the college I was attending got together and they made it possible for me to obtain psychological and diagnostic testing through the Office of Vocational Rehabilitation, because OVR then helps with rehabilitation.

"See, this is why God is so good. I took the tests, and the psychiatrist kept saying, 'If only someone had taken a little time with you when you were young, Samanda, things would be a little different for you. You're a very slow learner. I hate to tell you this, but you're not going to make it in college. You do not write well. In order to get through college, you will have to write well.' He gave me all these suggestions, different kinds of low skill, manual labor jobs I could do. 'You can work in a factory, you can work in a supply place for dental products, you can work in a grocery store or with food, but as far as working in an office or dealing with people, writing, you will not make it. The longer you go to school the harder it will be for you.' I had gotten my associate's degree then, and after what he said, I was going to stop school. But something told me, 'I didn't bring you this far to leave you.' And there was no way that I was going to give up. I have people all over this community helping me make it and I thank God for all of them. I learn mainly by hearing and doing. I put my notes on the tape recorder. And the more I hear it, the more I can understand it."

In a few months Samanda will graduate with a bachelor's degree in behavioral science. She plans to obtain a master's degree in social work. She is a full-time student, also working part time for the past two years with a social services agency as a supervisor of three group homes. She laughingly remarks that her friends ask her how she makes ends meet financially.

"I say, 'Well you know, I pay my tithes, which God gives me, and the rest, for some reason, it stretches, and it pays the rest of the bills. So that's God.'"

While a lot of people would not think about tithing if their resources were constrained, Samanda gasps, "Oh my goodness, if God gave me seventy, instead of seven, I'd give him seventeen. See that's me. Because I begged him to help me. And God has shown me when I give him the ten percent that's his, I am going to have ten percent for myself and something else. And this is what he's been doing ... he's been showing me out of the little money I make, he still provides for me. I thank God there's gas in my car, my car insurance is paid, and I have the school things I need. He just makes ways out of no way, and I'm not worrying about the money."

Samantha describes her most vivid memory from New Life. "We all had a love for one another. We talked about Jesus from the time we woke up 'til the time we went to bed. It was a wonderful experience meeting people from different cultures and coming together to worship under one roof. And it was amazing getting to know different sisters in the Lord and sharing their grief, their experiences, their abuse. As I graduated from the program I became a counselor—that's what made me want to go back to school. I wanted to reach out and give back what they had given to me."

A master's degree will allow Samantha to provide counseling as a professional. Longer term, her dream is to open a halfway house for girls who come out of prison. The type of program she envisions could also provide a transition from programs like NLFG to living and working full-time in the larger community and would be situated where there is greatest need: "I think the inner city community needs help more than other places, because that's where the people who are in the low income bracket live."

Samantha's idea of leisure activities is reaching out to others. "I enjoy doing street ministry." It is the type of open-air preaching and witnessing she first experienced in NLFG. "I remember how people were amazed at how the ladies would stand up and give their testimonies, describing what God had led them through, the different changes they went through, just to let someone else know that there's hope. If you are are some type of abuser, or you were abused, there's a way that you can get through that just by trusting and having faith in God. I do the same thing today with my church. We let others know that if you want to change, you can. You weren't born an addict. You can change if you believe."

There is a striking similarity between Samanda's story and Tawanda's dreams for her future. When Tawanda described how she learned to read in NLFG, she clapped and shouted, "My dream is finally going to come true! I'll get my GED, then go to nursing school, and eventually I'll own a restaurant. And have a husband. I'd like to have a kid before I'm forty-five." Tawanda grinned. "I would like to be able to bring my child to New Life for Girls, set him before God, say, 'Here's one for you.' I want to help the homeless with my restaurant. It's going to be for profit, but it's still going to be helping the homeless. The food that I would throw away at night I will give to the homeless instead. Now with the money that I make from selling my food, I would like to have a building, at the NLFG Chicago intro, for homeless persons. Let's say employment is down, if you get some of the men and women who are homeless together in one place and explain to them how to help the community, help themselves, help them build these abandoned buildings up, the abandoned homes up, that would stop some of the unemployment. Not only would it benefit the neighborhood, it would stop crime. That way they could earn money, pay their rent, we could take a lot of people off public aid, off the streets. Start with a small one first. Not a treatment program—that has to be voluntary. But they could see how we're living. Because a lot of people are not on drugs. There would be more places in the hospital for women who want to work as nurses. We could help them with daycare for their kids." Tawanda slaps her knee, pleased with her dream. "They oughta let me come to Congress to help!"

NINETEEN
BEAUTY QUEEN

Friday, June 14, 2002

*T*oday *three women make it to our Omega group meeting—Tawanda, Lupita, and Brooke. Kenda has to fold letters in the other
building; Sarah took her baby, Lea, to the hospital. Lea has been
very sick. (Tawanda, who begins the meeting with prayer, prays for
them.) Gisetta is now at Westminster, staff-in-training. Holly had to
do nursery duty.*

*Brooke brings her son (newly arrived) into the group from the
nursery because he woke up from a nap. So by the time we get organized (2:15) and break early (choir practice—which apparently
was canceled after all), we have just a half hour together and do not
discuss much. There are competing demands on time, so attendance
fluctuates. (Later, when I check attendance records for the entire seven
weeks, I discover that each Omega group participant missed the same
number of classes: two.)*

*A phrase Brooke uses in passing—beauty queen—reminds me of
how much these women have physically changed since they first entered New Life. They look healthier, cared-for. Their skin glows, and
their hair and clothing look fresh and clean. Changes in their outward
appearance reflect the changes in their inner life.*

*There are many beautiful women at New Life. The "beauty
queen" label surfaces for two in particular: Brooke, and a recent graduate named Dee, whom I met at an NLFG alumnae function. Even
the way in which the "beauty queen" label comes up for each of them
gives insight into its complex meanings.*

*For New Life residents, a label such as beauty queen holds shades
of meaning when they first enter the program and takes on a surpris-
ing new meaning as their perceptions change. At New Life I learned*

a lot from the residents about applying makeup and dressing stylishly, for starters. I have also been challenged to untangle the meanings threading their way through my own consciousness.

It is a paradox, this conflicted way women feel about their appearance: the most superficial of considerations on one hand and, because of its reflection of cultural milieu and its direct connection to identity, among the most profound and deeply rooted questions on the other. Some critics claim that a culture steeped in advertising and consumerism becomes toxic in its objectification of relationships and people, especially women.

Dee's spunky voice matches her cute appearance: short, stylish strawberry blonde hair framing a glowing smile of a face. She plucks her eyebrows, not unusual for women of New Life, who tend to pay careful attention to their appearance. Still, the concept of beauty queen does not surface until well into the conversation. She mentions that today is her birthday (she is forty, but looks younger). Dee does not need much prompting to talk.

Dee begins. "My current life, praise God, is just to do anything for his glory. The job that I'm currently in, it's like a secular job, I didn't go looking for any kind of Christian job so to speak, for the reason that I believe we need to be called into the world. He put me in the place I'm working at for a reason. I'm just trying to be in all things like Christ so I can make a difference. I started this job at a gravel pit, where there are a lot of truckers and men, but they know that I'm a woman of God just because of my behavior.

"I'm doing a lot of healing in my life. Sometimes on a day-to-day basis you can see the challenges that you face. You have a choice to feed into what the enemy has to offer or to make a difference in your own life. So I'm going to these healing seminars, and it's no coincidence that I've faced different difficulties on each day. But with Christ you can do anything. When you get on the other side you just feel more of the presence of God in your life."

Dee talks about the 18-week healing seminar sponsored by her church. "I was originally planning to go to school, but I changed my plans because I really felt as if I needed to heal some of my internal wounds. This SALT seminar can only be done with people who are dealing with sexual issues of some kind. The SALT acronym means, Sexual Addicts Learning Trust. The funny thing is, when I first moved up here I knew my brother was involved in something like that because of some past history he had. First thing I thought was, how can these people keep him in bondage like that? He had a problem with something in the family.

"To go back a bit, when I was thirteen I sat on my dad's lap because I wanted a hug. He was drunk and asked to see my breasts. That one incident changed everything. He didn't actually do anything, but I believe my brother almost did a similar thing with one of his stepchildren when he was drinking. As it turned out, one day I was visiting my niece, my brother's real daughter to whom this did not happen. She wrote her father a letter to explain her feelings. It was a hateful kind of letter, but on the other hand it was loving. I thought to myself, why can't she just let it go? I let it go with my dad when he hurt me. I thought I had forgiven him. And the Spirit told me, *Dee, you didn't let it go. You never dealt with your feelings, and at least she's dealing with hers.* I never dealt with mine, and that's why I drank and drugged for thirty years. I was blown away that the Lord talked to me in that way."

A central issue for many New Life women is trust, and Dee is no exception. "Trust is key because, ultimately, if you think back to childhood you suppress pain and build walls. When I was a teenager, I don't think I ever said that I wanted to grow up to be a drug addict. I'm sure I had higher hopes for myself, but that's what I turned out to be."

Dee describes the NLFG community. "Each person is important, and everybody plays a part in each other's lives. At NLFG, in second phase, you change rooms every month. I didn't dislike anybody. But sometimes you have a sandpaper sister, somebody who you know is going to be hard to live with, and more than likely if your heart doesn't want it, you'll probably get stuck with that person. But they are the ones that help you work out what you need. Because it's what's in you, the way you perceive her is what you have to deal with. God's hand is always in that. I can remember one particular person—she also just graduated recently—we would always tease each other about being sandpaper sisters. What happened was we had to live together *a second* month. We're dear friends today."

Recalling a vivid memory from her time at New Life, Dee connects her feelings about appearance and identity. "When I first got to Dover, it was the beginning of summer, I'll never forget. Everything was about change. You have to learn to deal with it. You have certain jobs as part of your program, and mine was to mop the kitchen floor before classes. I always had to have makeup on my face, always had to look pretty, before I was ready to go anywhere. I didn't know how to let myself be me. I was a nervous wreck, 'cause everything was always about me. If I looked good on the outside I thought I would feel better on the inside." She laughs. "The Lord was really looking through me. Anyway, to do the mopping job I had to finish by rinsing the mop out. Just then, the water ran out. Here I am with this dirty, smelly mop, yucky hands. I was in tears. The lady on duty said, 'Don't worry, there's bucket of water in the bathroom.' So I could at least wash my hands. She reminded me to do the work unto the Lord. I was mopping the floors for God. It was truly new to me. How important was it that I had to be pretty on the outside? Who was I going to sit in class with? A bunch of other girls! What was the big deal? God was showing me I had to deal with what's going on on the inside. I really didn't deal with a lot of my inside stuff until I left NLFG. All the classes do have to do with your issues, but I would always skim the surface of that stuff."

Dee did, however, observe changes in her identity while at New Life. Her expressive hands underscore her words as she speaks. "I was in high school with a lot of pretty girls, and you had to be a Barbie doll in order to be accepted. I was a wannabe, because everything was all about having a boyfriend. I wasn't really pretty enough. I always had bleached blonde hair, lots of makeup, and I was pencil thin, but I never liked my front teeth. I bought four caps for my teeth just a few years ago. I thought I had to look like all the girls on TV. It saddens my heart to think that's where my head was at."

Dee falls silent for a moment. "You know what's really special? During graduation last October they voted me, Miss Loving Caring Sharing. The girls voted for me!" She begins to cry. "It brought tears to my eyes and it's going to make me cry again. My whole life I thought I had friends. I was always a friendly person, but because of the way I appeared on the outside women couldn't get close to me. I didn't understand why they didn't like me. Then here I was at NLFG, and the Lord was telling me, 'I like you, Dee, for who you are.' I didn't have to have makeup, have my hair done. I was trying to figure out who I really was without the stuff on. When they voted for me, it was really a message from God."

Dee won the only prize awarded during New Life's graduation. "Miss Loving Caring Sharing" is a prize for inner beauty. As she tried to apply her new understanding of inner beauty in practical ways, she picked up another label from her NLFG friends: "At rec time at night, when we played Scrabble, someone would begin to gossip, and I would feel uncomfortable. One friend nicknamed me Edifying Dee. I think I really irritated her because I would press that issue. Looking back on it, it was hard for me to stand up for righteousness at times because friends are not always supportive. I can choose to sit here and play or I can leave. But she loved me anyway, and little by little it got passed around. By the grace of God the rest of my friends also caught that 'no compromise' attitude."

Another conversation underscores the radical difference between this understanding of beauty and the self-perceptions held by residents when they first enter NLFG. Long-legged, blonde Brooke—who could have been a beauty pageant contestant—describes herself, particularly in relation to men, while she was still drinking and drugging. "In high school I was never a reader, never into school. I was just there. I never really worried about being popular, I was never at the bottom, more like in the middle. I only associated with certain people, and even now I feel I'm withdrawing from everybody. I feel like I'm by myself, I've always felt alone. When I was using I was selfish. I didn't really care about anyone else's needs."

Brooke doesn't seem to have a sense of her inner worth. Her physical attractiveness is merely leverage in getting what she needs. "Right before I entered NLFG, when I was out on the street, I was at the bar and I was leaving with these younger guys. I left my purse and ID in their car and didn't even know them. Anyway, another guy came by, and he picked me up. It seems like when you're out there you just attract the drug addicts. We went back to his house. We did drugs. Afterward I thought I was going to die. I couldn't breathe. I was getting cold chills, and I couldn't even sit up or go to the bathroom. I peed myself. He must have been used to the stuff. I don't know if it had heroin in it, but it was so painful that I couldn't catch my breath. He was trying to have sex with me. I was in bed for a whole week, sweating, in pain, and still trying to smoke drugs! And I was numb. Now I know it was the Spirit telling me to stop. Something was going to happen, or I was going to die. I got up Friday well enough to get to the bar and get a buzz of alcohol. I partied Saturday and Sunday. By Sunday it was time for me to go. I just told this girl, 'I need to turn myself in.' She said 'Yeah, that's a good idea.' I was crying. I told these other people, 'This is it, I'm done.' You're hugging them, thinking they are your friends." She laughs derisively.

Brooke sees important changes in herself lately. "I have matured. I know I'm accountable for a lot of things. I'm learning how to deal with other people. Learning how not to judge. I never knew how to pray, and God is teaching me a lot. I spend a lot of time in prayer. New Life is not a program to me. God works, lets you know who you are, through the classes. It's about learning who you are and having a deeper relationship with God.

"I did a paper on Andrew, the quiet disciple. He was one-on-one, a background guy. He did the work, but people didn't know it. I've changed, but I'm still me. All the effort I put into drugs out there I'm using for good now. I always thought of myself as a humble person until I got here. Quiet. I'm the type of person who will go with the flow. Alcohol took me out of my shyness and made me more outgoing. Now I know humble means it comes from the heart. It's submission to God, doing his will. God is working a miracle in my shyness. I won't stop being quiet, but now I've got to get used to speaking out. I'm better at living it rather than talking it."

TWENTY
AWAKEN FROM THE DEAD

Friday, June 21, 2002

*T*oday all seven women show up for class They missed out on a trip to Pinchot Lake because of a staff note telling them to come here. They express a range of emotions from happy-to-be-in-the-group to I'm-here-because-I-have-to-be.

Tawanda can hardly contain her excitement when she arrives. "I received a revelation to intercede for the nations and stop my selfishness." A guest speaker today confirmed what she was praying, she adds. "Everyone at NLFG is a nation. Everybody here is from different backgrounds, with different needs, gifts, and nationalities. We are the body of Christ. I wept the whole day yesterday and pleaded, 'Take away my sinful urges and desires, Lord.' Today the speaker talked about 'Selah'—taking our thoughts captive. I was praying for God to change my judgmental heart. I've been judgmental. I catch myself doing it. I know it's wrong … it's me, me, me! Gimme God!" She rocks back in her chair, hands raised, looking triumphant.

Brooke catches Tawanda's excitement. "The gifts that each of us have been given will help us to minister. We all connect, because we're created in his image. Each of us is different, but we're going to minister based on what we've been through—be a nation to them."

Brooke sees herself as "that tree" we visualized in our previous discussion. She asks me to post the tree illustration so that the group can see it again. "We're going to be that image to someone, like the tree. The thickness is my strength, the courage that someone needs. Stability." Other group members chime in: "We'll be the branches that reach out to other people. The roots and the seed are what NLFG planted in our lives. The tree represents our new self image and identity!"

Community building holds a slightly different meaning for each woman. Brooke says, "When I go out I want to help women who are in the same position I was in. Give them hope. I don't want all this knowledge just for me. There's plenty of other people out there to minister to. I don't want to forget that I was on the streets with no food."

Brooke adds, "Working with the youth is important, and we should work with them young. I would like to bring God back into the schools."

Lupita says, "This reminds me of what Jesus did, with disciples, encouraging them to build. Jesus built trust and relationships. We can build gyms, so kids aren't in the streets. Bringing people together as one."

I label a fresh sheet of easel paper "Community Formation," and draw an arc-shaped line. I say, "Let's illustrate our theory of how community forms." I point to the left-hand side, marking the beginning of the continuum. "What is on this side, before community forms? Is that 'community'? 'No community'?" I ask.

"No, that's anti-community," Sarah says.

This is a term the group has used before to describe life in prison and on the streets. "Anti-community" does not surface much in the literature, and it is not well defined. The group has stumbled onto a new insight.

As the line arcs to the right, community forms and becomes stronger. Can it become too strong?

"Yes," several women respond. "That's a cult. They have community, but to the extreme."

Sarah clarifies, "There is overcontrol. Mormons don't allow exchange outside their community. You can't have companionship outside the cult. Husbands are picked for women. And Jehovah's Witnesses don't celebrate holidays."

A lengthy discussion ensues about the difference between occult and cult. After Kenda recounts being in an occult setting, the group agrees that members of the occult claim to worship Satan. Occult settings can also be cultlike.

Kenda describes her experience: "I worshipped Satan, even had a satanic bible. They had stores where you could get that in my community. Everything is the opposite of the Bible. It's very, very evil … and very easy to get into the group. They comforted me when I couldn't get help anywhere else. It was almost like a gang—easy to get in but hard to get out. You could die there."

That's how I felt in anti-community," Sarah says.

"In anti-community there's no hope," Kendra says. "You feel you're going to die. It's destructive. I went from cult to anti-community, to using drugs."

Sarah completes the contrast: "In a cult, there is uncertain hope. You don't know what your future holds. You could be reborn, for example, as a flower or a car."

The group reads two descriptions of community in the book of Genesis: The Garden of Eden (Chapter 2:8-25), and the Tower of Babel (Chapter 11) stories.

Sarah observes that the Tower of Babel story started out as community and went to anti-community. "They all got together and made bricks," Sarah says. "They could do anything they could imagine because they were of one accord."

Tawanda asks: "But what was their motive? Power! They wanted to get to heaven."

"Yes," says Sarah, "but it made them community."

Sarah and Tawanda disagree about when Babel became anti-community and why. Sarah says the reason God scrambled their speech was because they became powerful and cultlike, and when they could no longer communicate, fell into chaotic anti-community.

"They were trying to reach the heavens, because they wanted to feel significant," Holly says.

Tawanda adds, "They said 'let's make a name for ourselves' and they left God out of it."

The conversation moves on to the kingdom of God stories that Jesus tells in the New Testament. Matthew Chapter 13 includes a half-dozen different parables about the kingdom, in similes or word-pictures: The kingdom of God is like a mustard seed ... yeast ... treasure ... a merchant looking for pearls ... a net with all kinds of fish. In the parable of a farmer who goes out to sow his seed, some fell on thorns, where the seeds grew up but were choked. ("That's cult," several comment.) Some seed fell in rocky places, where they were scorched, had poor soil, no roots. ("That could be cult, or anti-community.") Some seed fell along the wayside, where birds ate them. ("Anti-community, death.") Some fell into the good soil and bore fruit. ("That's community!")

The women continue their animated discussion as they leave the library. Rosa drops by. She is no longer at the same point in the process as her peers, but she is interested in the Omega group and is willing to offer input. Often Rosa's perspective is refreshing in the midst of effusive God-talk.

Rosa is a stickler for truth and fairness. She doesn't like exaggeration. She layers words lavishly with a rapid-fire delivery in an earnest attempt to get descriptions exactly right. Rosa has had her own cult experience and her narrow escape from anti-community underscores today's discussion.

She settles into a chair in one corner of the library and tackles the question head-on.

"New Life is not a cult to me because they don't ask anything from you that you will lose. You are not being degraded, you are not being humiliated, and everything that makes you a person they try to develop through God. Being in a cult, my questions were never answered. When I got here, my ques-

tions were answered. Plus there's the fact that you can leave
anytime.

"A cult is different because they want to know everything
about you, every little thing. They use it against you. When I
walked in the cult I was very scared and insecure, having a lot
of nightmares, and not eating right. I was already sick before
I got there. Spiritually, I was sick and I didn't know it. I was
there for help, but they gave me half truths. The cult that I
was in, the main person was a witch." For months she was a
captive in a cult called Ma Dete Ma Wambo, which did not
represent itself as Christian.

"It was a whole different religion. They also called it La
Religion after three African goddesses. Even though the
leader was not black or African—she was this Puerto Rican
woman—the religion was based on African religion. I was living in New Jersey, and that religion is all over the Latino and
African communities. They take your money. When I walked
in that place it was full. It was a little apartment in the projects.
I think the whole atmosphere was cursed already. I have this
picture of the lady's eyes, and even now it spooks me. She was
all dressed in white and was *enyota*, crouched down, throwing
the *caracoles,* which are small seashells. That's how they talk to
the spirits. When I went in there her back was to me, but she
went like that"—Rosa crouches and turns abruptly, reenact-
ing the scene—"and looked at me. I just always remember
that look. It was a deep and hollow look, and it penetrated
me. She told me everything about the nightmares, my abuse,
my breakup with my fiancé, and the sickness in my ovaries.
I never asked any questions, never said anything. Then she
said, '*Rapide rapide. Corre, corre arriba,*' and like a fool I ran up
the steps." She laughs at her own foolishness. "I didn't even
know what she was going to do—they could have killed me.
'Hurry! Go upstairs to the bathroom,' she said. She gave me
the water baths, ripped my clothes with a knife, covered my
eyes with a blindfold, and then dressed me up and knelt me

down. She was throwing the *caracoles* as to how long I had to kneel down, what was going to be my name, and what spirits would be my guardians. I just stood there like a fool. I remember kissing the cross, a bone, and a knife.

"They cut you different places," Rosa says pointing to several places on her body. "They cut you on the bottom of your feet—not deep, because they don't want you to go. Once things start hurting you, you are already too brainwashed to leave."

Rosa rubs her eyes and leans back in her chair. "When that was happening, I didn't know what it was. I felt scared and cold like I was somewhere else. Something just hovers over you. It is creepy.

"At first it was free but later they began to demand money. The people that came to get help all had to pay. I was getting food stamps and welfare, and half of it was going to them. I was living with them and contributing. I was really gullible."

Rosa's identity in that setting was manipulated. The cult's leaders would discover points of vulnerablity and use them to control their followers. "I was very quiet, and I was also very thin. I weighed around eighty pounds, because after I had my daughter I fell into a very deep depression."

She sighs. "They drain you of yourself by giving you a personality trait based on spiritual guides—spiritual guides are doing something to you, that's why you're behaving like this. I already had a lot of rebellion and hurt against my mom, and they fed more into that. They had me thinking that my mother wasn't my mother. They had me thinking that my daughter was a reincarnation of the main goddess that they worshiped, and they separated my daughter from me. And then things just got bigger. They moved into a bigger house. Children were being born into it. The leader wasn't just dealing with the dead people or the dead spirits anymore, but with the saints. We also did voohidia, which is voodoo.

"We used to go into trances. At a certain level you might start *passando muentos*, which is the spirit of the dead person speaking through you. This cult was founded on different stuff, like *mesa blanca* (white table), *mesa negra* (black table), and *balaria,* which I don't know how to say in English. It was based on the dead spirits, and *santaria* was based on the saints. Sometimes there were bodyguards, like spiritual bodyguards, to make sure that no dead spirit would enter a person. The saints and the dead spirits didn't mingle, and a lot of bad stuff could happen.

"One time we were all in this house with a lot of new people there. There was a feast and everyone started going under, even the ones who weren't initiated yet. They started shaking and screaming and yelling. I remember the leaders arguing afterwards because it was out of control. One girl was trying to crawl out of the house, and she couldn't breathe."

Rosa looks at the "What Community Does" definition from the Omega Group, including the six metafunctions: sanctity, significance, safety, companionship, celebration, and exchange. "There was supposed to be sanctity in the cult," she states.

As for companionship and friendships: "In the beginning, they give you a sense of belonging and acceptance. Flattering words made you want to stay. At one time I thought I could do anything, and then the same confidence they give you, they tear up.

"It is a control thing. To break your spirit. You don't even know it's happening. Once I said to the leader, 'How come you don't ask people if they if want to be initiated?' She said, '*Es una cosa que no se pregunta.*' (You're not supposed to ask about that).

"Then I asked, 'What happens if we leave La Religion?' She said, 'You die.'"

Rosa decided to leave when she realized she was getting worse, not better. "I kept losing everything. I couldn't sleep.

That stuff was just tormenting me, and I thought I was going crazy. I'd always end up back in their home.

"They made it difficult for me to leave, but they were also throwing me out all the time. I was trying to do everything right so I wouldn't be homeless, or because I didn't want to be separated from my daughter. They had me sleeping with animals in the basement.

"Then they would do sacrificial stuff. It was terrible. I don't know why I stayed so long in that environment. I think I felt alone and crazy. I didn't know what else to do. That's when I started doing a lot of cocaine and alcohol. Yes, after I got sucked in I paid for it."

Rosa observes that the gay culture can also be cultlike: "You even feel rejection within the gay community. When I first came out and started hanging in that culture, my first lover was very boastful, it was a very powerful thing to be able to say that she turned women to the gay lifestyle. And then it was like I was prey—fresh meat—everybody wanted to get their claws in me. It was crazy. Then you fall into it. I would look for women that had never been with a woman before so that I could turn them out. You learn that and it's a whole culture. You go to the gay clubs, you go to the gay restaurants, everything you go to is gay, gay, gay because that's where you were accepted, that's where you were wanted, that's where you were needed."

Rosa knew she was coming into a Christian program when she first arrived at Westminster. Her walls were up. "I was a basket case when I arrived. I have been able to think step-by-step what happened. I feel at ease when things make sense to me. I can actually say, 'Well forget it.' I was never able to do that. I would just add to my own internal myths of why life wasn't fair."

Rosa pauses, shifting her train of thought. "The first time I was here for all the wrong reasons. It was hard. I don't like being around a crowd of people. It felt suffocating—too big, too loud, too much. I wasn't ready. I told that to Dennis. Too much, too big. And because I was surrounded by so many women, I was scared that I wouldn't be able to control my hormones and I would get caught.

"In intro, I was kind of attracted to someone, but it faded because we were all there for the same reason. The last thing I was thinking about was sex, but then when I came to Dover, I did struggle. That was what I wanted to avoid, but in a way it was good. I was guilty because I was feeling attraction. But I said, 'Wait a minute, I'm not doing anything wrong. And the person is not doing anything wrong either.' And then I tried not even looking at the person. But that wasn't fair to the person or to me. So I started looking at her and talking to her as my sister in Christ. As time went by, it just kind of stopped."

By the second time she came to Dover she was more prepared. "I was willing, but I don't know if I was ready. I was trying harder, and that in itself was something different. I didn't try to change at first. You hear, 'God is going to change you.' So, I'd be like, 'okay, so change me.'"

Rosa laughs. "Nothing happened. Because I realized you have to put an effort to it. Surrendering and submitting. If you don't do that, you're not going to grow. And sometimes you have to confront. But mostly I give it to him. Because every time I try to do it myself, I do it wrong.

"I am trying to learn a new way." Rosa stands to stretch. She glances at the shelves lined with books, pointing out books that she has read. She sits down again and sighs. "I'm lazy, too—that has something to do with it. Sometimes I wait until a certain situation gets real bad, then I call out to God. That's not fair either. I need to maintain contact with the Holy Spirit. Everything that I do, I have to give to him. I'm realizing that. I found that I'm a very selfish person." She repeats "selfish" in a whisper, then laughs. "Even in the good things I'm a selfish Christian. I find myself thinking, 'I'm going to graduate, go to college, then get a car.' All this material stuff. God may not want that. My dreams, hopes have to be centered on him. I still have to give up—and I haven't—still have to give up those dreams in my life."

Rosa says that community for her is a network of relationships, but she didn't understand the function of community at NLFG at first. "The first time I came here I thought it was a program, and I didn't understand what this had to do with my alcohol problem. I knew it was a Christian program, but I thought the resources were just to help you to get rid of your addiction. I thought it was going to be just counseling sessions. And I could deal with the dishes, cleaning, even getting up early. But I couldn't understand why we had to have church. What did that have to do with my addiction?

"The second time I had such a sense of family. I felt that I was loved, and that I was getting something new. Now, sometimes, I see certain things coming out of my personality that are pure. And I think, 'Wow, that's nice.' I'm caring again. When I was growing up I was caring, I loved people and just wanted to help them. Then I went to the extreme of hating people. I see the caring coming back. I think it's God surfacing in me. I just get scared of being hurt or rejected. But then I fear so much hating people the way I did. I don't want to be like that. I question myself, 'Are you willing to care enough to get hurt?' I think it was the Holy Spirit that told me that everyone else was here for the same reason. That gave me compassion for them. They were all hurting. The addiction adds on to your hurt in the sense that you do things you would not ordinarily do. I never thought that I would betray a best friend. But I did. I never thought that alcohol was gonna hold me down to the point and I was going to do things I would be ashamed of."

Rosa walks upstairs to her dorm room. She gathers a framed photo of herself arm-in-arm with her daugher and smiles back at the pair of happy faces, so much alike.

"My relationship with my daughter is very important because I've come to realize that she was so wanting me to love her. When I showed her affection I was always drunk. So that little bit of love that I showed her she just soaked it up. When she came here for the two weeks, she pushed me away, and I was hurt. She doesn't know how to react, because she sees that I'm sober, and she doesn't have to soak up the leftovers. She's not a baby, she's twelve. And it's been almost a year since we've been separated—that alone will change her character."

She continues, "And when I think about my daughter I think I don't even know her. She was telling me she wanted to be a vet." She laughs. "I said, 'Oh, that's cool.' But she wants to be a model, too. I said, 'Well you be a model and then you can pay for veterinarian school. It's going to be expensive to learn how to operate on animals.' She said, 'Operate on the *animals*?'" Rosa imitates her daugher's surprise, then breaks up laughing. "I said, 'What did you think, you were going to play with the animals all day?'"

Rosa adds, "I sometimes think even a person who is not looking for God would benefit from a program like this. Because they know what they lack in their life by the time they leave. But they have to be willing. Even if they come just to get clean, like I did, and they end up leaving, not finishing, they already know what's lacking in their life. Even if they leave not accepting God, or because they think they're ready, they leave knowing in their heart what's lacking. When you get to NLFG, you're tagged." She taps her visitor on the shoulder in an imaginary game of tag and shares another laugh.

On the dark drive home I think about how I want the best for Rosa, and all of the women I have met at New Life. Although this is a natural response for any thinking, feeling human being, it creates potential dilemmas for the researcher, which requires that I have big ears and eyes and a guarded tongue. In participant–observer research, the researcher practices "empathy neutrality"—empathy toward the participants, neutrality in regards to outcomes and findings. For the research, I posed the same set of questions to participating residents and alumnae.

After completing the research on community building and the power of relationships in organizations, I realize that the lives of these women, men, and children still represent an important and powerful untold story.

So I return to the material in the role of a storyteller—just as Tawanda and the other women predicted and hoped that I would. As I review my interviews with alumnae, a pattern emerges: Their stories dovetail dynamically with residents' stories, and they become my way of imagining the positive futures of New Life's current residents.

Mercedes is a 1979 graduate of New Life whose story could represent Rosa's future. She now works for a college in its finance department and is the sister of a current staff member. At age forty-six, Mercedes is vivacious and well spoken and, also like Rosa, of Puerto Rican descent.

"My husband and I have been married for twenty-four years. He is a graduate of Teen Challenge," she offers. Her most vivid memory of NLFG was of being separated from her children. "At the time I went through the program, children were not allowed to live with you on the main campus. They were on what they called the children's farm. It was winter and often snowfall would keep us from seeing our children. There were times when I could not see my children for two months, and that was the hardest thing that I went through. My children absolutely adored the mountain. To this day they still—and they are both in their twenties—talk fondly of their life at New Life.

"After graduation, my husband and I immediately became staff. We worked there until 1981. We moved to Chicago and then came back in 1983 and worked there five more years. I also had little odd jobs; I was a counter girl at a dry cleaner the whole time I was there.

"My husband and I met in the streets. We were strung out together, and we lived together before we entered the program. We had our two children, then he went to Teen Challenge and I came to NLFG. We got our act together and we got married after we graduated. I would say probably 90 percent of my current friends at some point have been associated with New Life."

Mercedes says NLFG is an intimate community, even a "large extended family of some kind. I still enjoy spending time with them. You know what I mean, they understand, I guess. I'm not sure how to describe what that feeling is other than it's about the people, relationships, but also the shared experience.

"Now I work in a college, out in the country. I have friends here, but a lot of people don't even know what my life was all about. It's not that I'm trying to hide it, it's just that I don't think a lot of people understand. There are very few people I can completely open up with.

"I live in an area that is very rural, and these are people who have lived here all their lives. I could very well be misjudging them, but I don't want to take that chance. These people don't even know what drugs are all about, and some of them don't even want to drive on the highway because they're afraid. They won't go into the city. If they won't even take those steps, there is no way they'll understand why I did the things I did and how I was able to change and be who I am today. But there are some people who grew up out here who totally understand. It takes a while to be open and honest about your life. That's why the sense of community, with my church and with NLFG, is so important. There is no holding back. They know from beginning to end who I am." Mercedes flushes with excitement when the conversation turns to her family and her future plans.

"I am almost finished with a master's degree in counseling. Only two more classes. Then I want to get my licensing.

Hopefully, be able work in the field. I enjoyed my work at New Life immensely. My children have always encouraged me to keep striving. My daughter and I got our undergrad degree together. They put it in the local newspaper. It was so much fun, and I'm glad I did it because it also makes them work. My daughter has her master's in social work. My younger son is just finishing up and moving right along, which is great. When I left New Life in 1988, I started taking classes. It took twelve years, but I did it.

"As for the future, I tell people I don't know what I'm gonna be when I grow up," Mercedes laughs. "I know that I really enjoyed working at New Life, but I know that I could not do that now. It's very intense to live on the property and be there constantly. I don't think I have that in me anymore. But I would like to work with teenage girls who have become pregnant. I was there once and I know where they're coming from. I don't really know if I will go back into drug and alcohol counseling. Perhaps counseling in a community health center setting, I have been praying with friends at church about that possibility."

Mercedes believes watching out for one another is what NLFG is all about. "It's making sure everybody's okay, 'cause things happen constantly; you're dealing with people's lives twenty-four hours a day, seven days a week. There are few times when you can breathe and say things are okay right now. It's a constant watching out for each other."

She came to faith because someone was there to pick her up. "I was seven months pregnant with my daughter, and the same friend who brought me into the program took me to church. I accepted Jesus in church while I was strung out and pregnant." Mercedes laughs, remembering. "I would be high and sitting in church, but she faithfully took me. Then after the baby was born a year later she told me about the program."

After a long pause she says quietly, "It was a life-changing experience. I just know that if it wasn't for New Life..." she begins to cry. "I look at my life and realize how tremendously blessed I am. If it had not been for New Life and people willing to give of themselves for me and my family I know I wouldn't be here today.

"My back was up against the wall. I had kids and nowhere to live. I'd been thrown out of my apartment, out of every relative's house. There was nowhere to take my children. And I was so strung out I could barely feed them anymore. My girlfriend was at the point where she told me I had to either go in the program or she would call the Bureau of Child Welfare. I probably would have ended up dying—that's the way I was going.

"It's amazing, it really is. Sometimes you don't think about it, and when you do remember back, you think, 'Wow, look where I was twenty-five years ago, and look where I am today.' What a blessing, what a gift I've been given!"

TWENTY–ONE
UNMASKED

Sunday, July 7, 2002

This last meeting requires more preparation—certificates of recognition, detailed agenda, two sets of handouts, a set of community building circles, and sticky notes for each woman.

Everyone attends. Holly brings her son. He's noisy and frets almost the entire time. Tawanda helps Holly with him.

In a previous session, the group was able to describe anti-community and cult, in terms of the absence or extremes of the metafunctions of community. Today they use the metafunctions to generate a rich anthropological description of NLFG.

Under *exchange* Sarah lists babysitting, and Tawanda suggests the individual jobs.

For *safety* Holly says, "Doors are locked at night." Brooke adds, "We're set apart from the world, protected. This is all safety. We're not even allowed to watch certain TV programs; it's 24-hour Christian programming."

Celebration is another of the metafunctions. "We celebrate everything," says Sarah. "The Fourth of July, cookouts, fireworks, Hershey Park, birthdays."

Moving on to *sanctity* Kenda contributes, "We have quiet time—fifteen minutes for devotions; it's mandatory." Sarah agrees. "That's our main metafunction. Anything after fifteen is voluntary, but students often stay for hours and hours."

Brooke chimes in. "After the Emmanuel stage, there is more flexibility, but you must make your own time. It's a transition from mandatory to voluntary."

Tawanda explains, "It's like, 'Now that we have shown you, what are you going to do with it?'" The first time she was here she did not do the voluntary devotions when given freedom, but this time she is.

For the metafunction *significance* Sarah comments, "We are taught by the Word of God that we're all important, God loves us all the same, and no one's more special than anyone else. When we do something wrong, they take us into the office and explain it, they don't just throw us a discipline. They let *us* try and suggest things that will help us. At the same time they use both discipline and love."

They compare New Life with that of other programs.

"The others don't give you love," Brooke states. "You can tell they just do it for money."

Sarah adds, "That's another thing. They don't get paid here. They receive a missionary's salary, which is twenty dollars or something like that. So you know they do it out of love. Definitely not for money."

Under *companionship* Holly lists new friends. Sarah elaborates, saying, "Any relationship here is meaningful; on the streets the whole point of our relationships was to use or be used. Now it's more to give than to receive. And be compassionate to one another. Love each other."

Each participant gets a pad of sticky notes and a set of circles, graduated in size. They are invited to come up with more examples of how the metafunctions appear at NLFG, as many as they can generate, and to list each separately on the stickies. The women think about what they do, or what they see others doing. Next, they are invited to attach the sticky notes of attributes to the circles of various sizes and play with them, arranging them in meaningful ways.

The women generate dozens of NLFG descriptors for each metafunction of exchange, and Kenda beams as she realizes that she came up with the most.

Referring to their use of the circles, the group discusses

the relative size and interrelationships of the metafunctions.

Sarah remarks, "Sanctity is the largest group for New Life." And Lupita says, "We celebrate Jesus with beautiful smiles."

Looking at the circle patterns they have made, they note a clear link between sanctity and celebration. That may surprise the outside world.

Tawanda: "Exchange is big."

"And companionship, too," Brooke adds.

Says Sarah, "Here at New Life we're taught that God keeps us safe. Anytime we go anywhere we pray for safety. We pray for our food." Tawanda agrees, "We lay hands on one another, for healing." Sarah interjects, laughing: "And no hitting or fighting!" Lupita adds, "Sisters argue. You have that in any family. But deep inside, we're all true friends. We're not passing drugs, we're passing Bibles, Scripture. If we do argue we end up hugging and saying we're sorry. That's what's so important about this program. Everybody learns to love each other as one family. The devil will attack us, get us to do other things. When I first got here to Dover I felt safe knowing that Jesus would take good care of me here."

The women think it is possible to have too much of any of the metafunctions.

"Celebration, busy schedules—we get tired," says Sarah. "Again, sometimes we need more sanctity, time to relax." Tawanda agrees, saying, "You can get burned out. We're up fifteen or sixteen hours a day—sometimes twenty. Constantly going. We don't get enough sleep."

The subject of subgroups at NLFG comes up. In the past it has been a hard conversation for everyone.

Sarah says, "Sometimes some people get into groups, where they will hang out with certain people. I think that, for the most part, we all change who we sit with and hang out with. In some classes our assignment is to do that. We're not allowed to get into cliques. They want the emphasis to be on God, not on your group."

*I introduce the concept of "boundary spanners": people with the abil-
ity to relate to different groups, to penetrate boundaries of smaller
groups for the benefit of the larger group. Are there boundary spanners
at New Life?*

Sarah says, "Definitely. I had my ideas, my set way of thinking
when I came here. It's pretty much all changed. (The group
laughs, in agreement.) I have opened up my boundaries to
teachers and to the counselors here. Opened myself up to
new ideas. I wanted to change, I wanted to be different."

*We wrap up the hour with oral and written evaluations of our time
together. Staffer Mary offers to take the group on a celebratory trip to
a nearby ice cream shop, so we climb into the van. Holly asks us to
bring back a soda for her. Our chatter and laughter compete with the
van engine as it winds its way into town. We buy our ice cream and
find two picnic tables under a massive oak tree's cool shade.*

*Mary and I co-present the certificates I have printed for each
Omega Group member, commending their participation. I call out
each name, and Mary hands the participant her certificate. We shake
hands with each woman. Their faces glow with the pride of accomplishment, and they exclaim over the colorful graphics and recognize
images and symbols (a tree, circles) from our time together.*

*As it happens, Kenda's certificate is the last to be presented. "The
last shall be first!" she crows, joined by the laughing shouts and applause of her peers.*

*The easy conversation continues as women share new insights
from our class, or reminisce about NLFG experiences. The conversation does not depend on or revolve around Mary or me, though we
listen and participate in the banter across the tables. I sense that we
have "lifted the mask" perhaps as much as any group can, in ways
that are deeply meaningful.*

TWENTY-TWO
NEW LIFE GRADUATION

Saturday, October 26, 2002

*T*he directors inform me when I arrive at graduation, I will be made an honorary graduate. Lily escorts me to her office for a cap and gown. My husband and a friend of ours have come along to videotape the graduation. The Westminster director approaches me, flashing his Cheshire cat grin: "Honorary graduate, eh? Congratulations! You are one of only ten!"

During the ceremony the director announces that there is an honorary graduate not listed in the program. Introducing me, he explains that NLFG allowed me to live with them as a resident for my doctoral research. The same tumultous shouting and applause that greeted every other graduate now greets me. As I walk up the center aisle of the auditorium my husband's face merges with hundreds of others, cheering me on. I reach the microphone, where I say a few words, as the others have done.

I thank the graduates, the staff, and the board of New Life for allowing me to be a part of the program and part of the graduation. I explain that the research is an in-depth study of a community-as-organization, and that residents, staff, and alumnae served as co-researchers. A key difference of this "program," I say, is that the women who leave are equipped for servant leadership at a time when we desperately need such leaders. I say that I am proud to be an honorary member of the graduating class of 2002. Then I turn to salute them.

It is a moment perfectly preserved in the amber of my memory.

In one sense, graduates of New Life never really leave. That's the thing about a genuine community, where the miracles of love and caring happen every day. Once you have tasted it, you hunger for it. Wherever you go in the world, the spirit of community stays with you, an ever-present reminder of what can be. A morsel of eternity. A blessed addiction.

In the corridor leading to the auditorium, the nineteen graduates nervously wait to have their names announced. They are lined up by height.

They struggle to maintain their composure.

The face of each graduate is radiant, framed by a gold tassel, white cap and gown. They look like women who are ready to begin the rest of their lives. Some of them will accomplish what they say they will and more, without ever returning. Some will return, victorious, wanting to stay connected with this place. Some will return limping and leave again restored. Some will languish anonymously.

I have no way of knowing for certain how any of them will fare, although I have confidence in all of them, my sandpaper sisters. What I do know is that each one is willing to share the secret knowledge she has about our communities, our organizations, our congregations, and ourselves. Whether anyone listens, time will tell.

TWENTY-THREE
THROUGH THE LOOKING-GLASS

*I*t *is a moonless night on the evening I call Wendy. My office window frames the shadowy silhouettes of trees and a meager patch
of stars.*

*Wendy and I are three years apart in age. At first it is difficult
for me to imagine this attractive, 45-year-old professional woman
as a 16-year-old addict, newly arrived at New Life back in 1974.
When she answers the phone, her voice sounds youthful. She is able
to capture the nuances of her experience so expressively that I can see
the girl she was, sneaking cigarettes in the woods between attempts
to run away.*

Wendy describes a typical day in her work as a licensed outpatient drug and alcohol counselor. "I get up in the morning,
make sure I'm mentally and spiritually prepared for the day.
I go to work, I see drug and alcohol clients all day in my office on an outpatient basis, and I also go to the local prison
and do drug and alcohol evaluations and assessments there.
I work with anybody in the family who's affected by drug
and alcohol addictions; sometimes that's children, sometimes
spouses, and others. Not only does that mean actually talking with people, but there is a lot of paperwork. The facility
where I work is a licensed drug and alcohol facility so there's
a lot of requirements and paperwork to keep updated. That's
how most of my day is spent. Depending on how long the
day is, when I go home I spend time doing things that need
to be done at home. My 20-year-old daughter lives with me.
Sometimes on Thursday nights we go to a Bible study and
after the study we go out on the streets and talk to kids who
are addicted to heroin or living on the streets—but that's kind

of a hobby thing," she laughs, recognizing that it's an unusual hobby. "That's a day in the life of Wendy."

She pauses, remembering. "I was sixteen when I was a member of NLFG, but I think one of the greatest memories I have from that time is just living in an atmosphere where I felt cared about and safe. Safe from myself, my addiction, and from others using drugs. I felt loved and very, very supported."

At New Life, Wendy made a startling discovery about herself. "One specific story that I use a lot in conversations with clients is how, after being sober for a couple of months, I realized that I didn't really have any kind of personality. I know that sounds kind of strange, but the best way I can describe it is that I was blank. I had no opinion about anything because I had spent four years doing nothing but the drug culture thing. So I was afraid of people, afraid of having conversations with people. If someone sat next to me my hands would sweat, and my stomach would cramp up. I didn't know how to handle a conversation without depending on a drug. At that time there was a barn at NLFG, and I spent a lot of time out there because I didn't know how to be around people. I remember being out there praying, crying to God. I wasn't even sure how to pray, but I asked him to give me a personality. I promised that if any opportunity came up where anybody thought that I had any hope to offer them I would let them know the Lord did a work inside of me, because I was incapable of doing that myself. And that was a pivotal turning point for me. After that I had to make myself be around people, and it was uncomfortable, I had to push through that wall, and pray and wait and see how God would show up and help me handle my anxiety. It took a long time, but I tell this story to my clients who have depended on drugs or alcohol for socialization."

Such radical change takes time, she admits with a chuckle. "I would say probably a good six months. And then the anxiety left as I got to know people and the environment remained the same—that kind of helped with building trust. I think dealing with my self-confidence took years. God answered the prayer, and now people can't shut me up." She laughs.

Wendy works with a broad array of clients: "I really cannot say that there's any person or situation that I'm not comfortable with. At one particular prison where I work, there are men who are child molesters, and that's always one of the most challenging populations to work with—especially for women. It was uncomfortable at first, but I went back to the Lord and said, 'You love these people the way you love me; give me your heart for them.'"

She pauses, weighing her thoughts carefully before continuing. "One of the reasons why it is difficult for me is because I am a survivor of sexual abuse. When I first went over to the prison I had a lot of anxiety, very similar to the anxiety I felt way way back when I was spending time in the barn alone. I went in very guarded, with the intention of just doing my job. Just get the drug and alcohol information; get in get out." She laughs, remembering. "But something happened between the guard gates. I asked the Lord to help me see this person the way he saw him. I knew I was incapable of doing that myself.

"The room where I work is right next to the guard station; it is safe. When I sat down at the table, this young man came in. He sat down in front of me, and I looked in his eyes; I experienced God's love coming into me—it was something not of myself—and I was able to truly see him as a very hurt, and, in this case, a very ill individual. It was grace that I experienced, and compassion. The anxiety totally left. I was able to do what I needed to do. More than that, I had the opportunity to reassure him that there is a God who loves him in spite of anything he had done or anything that was done to him. It was powerful."

The conversation turns to community.

"When I hear that word, it reminds me of family, and not necessarily blood relatives. To me it means commitment, it means one person doesn't do anything alone, and it means that we join together to accomplish whatever the goal is; that could be anything from helping someone move to being with someone having a baby who doesn't have anyone to support her, to vacuuming for someone who has had surgery and can't do that. So, to me, community means family and commitment, and there's no end to it.

"So, New Life for Girls is a community. Absolutely. In the sense that, well, some of the common obvious things are that everybody's living there together in a close proximity. But it's also a community in the sense of being there for one another, whether it's staff for staff, students for students, or any combination together. Members hold similar goals: wellness, healing, wholeness."

Having a circle of friends, a deep, rich set of relationships, has become increasingly rare in our society, Wendy observes. "It takes commitment. When things are difficult in the relationship it's because you're that involved in people's lives. I mean, it's easy to go to church and it's easy to attend a meeting, but it's not easy to be available the best I can be. What becomes challenging in community—and this happens at NLFG—is when you're that closely involved with other people there are times when there's all kinds of guardedness; walls come up. We don't want people to know things, and we want to hide that we're hurting. When you're in relationships with a small group of people in this way, you're constantly faced with the decision to run and hide," she laughs, "or take a risk and just be vulnerable and go through the pain of misunderstanding rather than running or bailing out. That's the challenge of NLFG, when everybody is living together, different cultures, belief systems, backgrounds. It's easy when you go to chapel services and everybody is worshiping; it's difficult when you go back to your room and your roommate borrows something and hasn't asked for it. In that mix it's more complicated than, say, attending a corporate meeting. The idea of community gets challenged in the nitty gritty kind of dirty, ugly places. Really tested.

"Because when you're living in that environment you can only hide in the barn so long"—laughing—"before somebody starts realizing it. Living in that small environment you're forced to push through. When I was there it was a tiny, tiny little house, and there were twenty-some people at Dover. There were no introduction centers. It was so crowded—we had 5-minute showers. There's only so much running away and hiding from yourself and other people that you can do. The schedule's so tight that you're forced to be with people most of the day anyway. You have to drop the wall and start to get real with somebody, because there's no place to hide." She chuckles. "Somebody's there *all* the time."

Wendy was a resident when NLFG had just opened its doors and could describe what had changed, and what remains the same. "When the girls came off the street we would show them the ropes, explain the routine, and also pray for them so they wouldn't experience withdrawal from the drugs. And if that meant that we stayed up all night that's what we did. When we had Bible classes, we started out with the agenda for the day. There were several times the director came in to teach a class, and I remember opening in prayer and it seemed like God wanted to do something other than just teach the class. So we would spend time talking and praying and interacting with each other about issues that were current at that time rather than sticking with the agenda. We had a lot of flexibility that way.

"Counseling was quite different. There was no structured peer or individual counseling time. My understanding is they didn't have the paperwork or the regulations that needed to be followed back then. If you needed to talk to somebody

you could go to a counselor day or night. And most counseling centered around teaching, sharing, praying, and being
there. It wasn't real 'professional,' but it was genuine and there
was concern and care. I suppose the structure is pretty much
the same as now.

"We had a variety of counselors. There were a couple of
college students who were doing internships, a couple of
Mennonites, but most of the staff were not recovering except for the founding and current directors. There were a few
graduates but not many; I was one of the first graduates on
staff. For me, if I had a problem or a situation that was both-
ering me, I would not seek out a recovering person. If I had
the choice between someone who had graduated or someone with no background, I went to the person who had no
background. At that time, I felt, and I still feel this way actually
in some respects, there was more tenderness, openness, caring, genuineness from the people who hadn't been through it;
they were more open rather than jumping to, 'Well here's what
happened to me, so here's how you should do it.' They were
more inquisitive, listening, asking more questions. Sometimes
that kind of response is a function of how long someone has
been in recovery. When they're newly recovered there's a lot
of, 'Oh I have all the answers, let me save you.' That's a turn-
off." Wendy chuckles. "It is part of recovery, though, because
you go from one extreme—feeling like you're nothing—to
'Now I know everything.' I would say someone who has been
delivered from addiction offers better quality of care after
they've been sober and clean a couple years, and preferably
if they leave and come back. There's a whole different type
of comfort, guidance, and advice after you have left a serene
and safe environment, gone to the 'real world,' and then come
back."

Since Wendy has experience in a variety of treatment
settings including faith-based, she can discuss differences in
treatment approaches. "Secular curriculum and religious cur-

riculum for treatment are vastly different. They are not alike in any way. Except for the fact that people are in a group. Secular programs—drug and alcohol education, addiction education, talking about what you used to do, the mental effects of drugs, about your family, what they did—NLFG is nothing like that. It's Bible classes. Talking about who you are in Christ and your values in the Lord. Understanding what's in the Bible, how it works and how you apply it. Completely opposite. The rule at NLFG is you don't talk about the street unless you're in counseling and you have some specific purpose for it. Whereas in secular program that's what we do all day long, talk about our experiences on the street."

I wonder if she is suggesting that one approach tends to work, and one tends not to; I ask her to respond as if talking to a "secular" audience.

Wendy clarifies an oft-asked question: What treatment approach works? "First of all define 'work.' Does it mean sobriety? If that's the case, then secular treatment offers that, and some people actually get sober. So in that sense it works. It's not for everybody. But it doesn't work for everybody in Christian treatment either. It depends on what 'work' is. So if you look at it as being about sobriety, then both types can offer that. But is the end goal to be drug and alcohol free, or to have some sort of purpose and direction for life? In many secular programs the goals are to learn how to not use drugs, how to maintain a stable job, and how to get back with your family. That's it. And that's okay and better than dying or killing yourself on the street or in your family relationships. But I think there's a deeper layer than just being sober. The difference between quitting drugs and recovery. Some people quit drugs, but their characters don't change. They still act like jerks; they're still disrespectful to themselves, to others. 'Act like a jerk' is not very clinical, but … "

She laughs, then continues.

"There are character defects that come with the lifestyle of substance abuse. So some people can quit. Quit. But that's different from looking inside your life and reconciling mistakes, facing and dealing with pain that you've been running from. Relationships, restoration, redemption. You're talking about character. There's a big difference between not using drugs and having a whole life change. If I were to speak to a mixed group about the differences between secular and Christian recovery, I would say that both offer help in different senses, and if the goal is to get sober and have some sort of leveling out of life, then pick. If your goal is to have a new life, a whole different perspective no matter how hard that may be, then you might want to consider Christian treatment because it's totally, radically different. I would also offer the statistics from the "Jesus factor" studies versus the very sad statistics of repeats, people going in and out of rehab. But it's really up to the individual what they want." She concludes, "Without God at the center of NLFG it would just be another inpatient program. If it weren't for the spiritual part you could spend twenty years there and walk out and fall on your face."

The topic shifts to referrals, and how people become aware that there are faith-based treatment options. "As a drug and alcohol counselor employed at a secular drug and alcohol licensed facility, most of the people who come in don't have any spiritual roots, and most don't have any interest in it. Part of my job is assessing what they are open to and want or need, and how far they're willing to go for recovery. And I try to encourage the ones who are open at all to seriously consider Teen Challenge or NLFG because I think they offer the most. But when that happens—say a heroin addict who is open to NLFG—they need to be detoxed first. I send them for detox, because there aren't any Christian detoxes that I'm aware of in my area. In the detox program they are pushing treatment goal, and most detox centers do not consider Teen Challenge or NLFG to be a real program. They will often sabotage what we've already put into place. I think they feel that way because of the religious emphasis; they are of the mindset that addiction is a disease and that's it. They don't have the belief or training to think there is a way, other than AA or other 12-step program, to attain a different life. That's just how they're trained.

"So, in the past few years, if I have someone in that situation, I go to Christian families who are willing to let the person detox in their homes. I have physician's assistants who will work with me and prescribe medicines for the symptoms of detox; they do the blood work and all the physical stuff. I have the family sign a contract, and I have the client agree. Like NLFG, there can be no telephone calls or going anywhere. So they must agree to this. The whole burden is not on one family; we try to find other believers who can volunteer some time to relieve them, watch a movie, talk. Usually it's in a country setting because that works much better."

I ask Wendy for a definition of detox.

"Detoxification," she clarifies, "is the critical physical withdrawal from an addicting substance—narcotics, barbituates, and alcohol, predominantly. The idea is to not have any of that in their system, or be going through withdrawal, at the time they go to intro. That has to do with licensing and liability. There is no real threat with heroin withdrawal. You may feel like you're going to die, but there are no seizures or things like that, which are risks associated with alcohol and barbituate withdrawal."

Wendy says it was her high school psychology teacher who referred her to NLFG after hearing about the program through his church. "He didn't have any choice—I was drool-

ing on my test and falling off my chair," she laughs. "He knew
the Lord and knew I was in bad shape. He and his wife took
me to a lot of church activities.

"I was raised in a Methodist church. Went there from the
time I was born. I knew I was in trouble, and I went to my
minister for help. He was taking me to interviews at other
drug treatment places. At one point, he told me was taking
me to a treatment place and he raped me. After that I didn't
go back to him or have anything to do with any church. Then
after my psychology teacher started talking to me, another
student invited me to church and I went to hers; it was non-
denominational. At that church I turned my life over to God.
It was a couple of weeks before I entered NLFG. I didn't go
to church on any regular basis because I was still walking in
my addiction. That was my faith background, but I never ever
knew that it was anything more than just going to church. I
had a slip after I graduated when I was seventeen or eighteen.
I haven't abused substances since."

*I turn off the tape recorder, and we say our goodbyes. For some reason
I add, "It was hard for me to hear you describe being raped by your
pastor."*

*She must have noticed something in my voice, because instead of
simply acknowledging my comment, she asks, "Why was it hard for
you to hear that?"*

*I feel the anger rise in my voice as I respond, "It just makes me
angry that a man, especially a pastor, would betray your trust and
hurt you like that." She assures me that she has recovered, and that
she has forgiven him.*

*We are silent, as if waiting for something. She asks me, gently,
"Michele, has someone hurt you?"*

*To my astonishment, her question releases in me a torrent of
dammed-up emotion. I begin to sob. I tell her about being raped by
a boyfriend in college. And about being propositioned by a professor.
I tell her, "No one knows except my husband and adult sons." As*

I weep, other injustices, long submerged, come to light: the missions agency leader who came on to me. About how I told my then-pastor, who refused to believe me. The emotional and physical pain of those assaults pales in comparison to my sense of injustice, the betrayal of not being believed. Through their abuse of power and position, they attempted to make me invisible and obliterate my identity, greedily gobbling it up: the oysters' fate in Tweedledee's verse. I am angry with myself for having kept their secrets.

Wendy offers to pray. I do not recall any details of the prayer, or what she says to me when we finally say goodbye.

What I do experience is an incredible lightness of spirit. As an-other alumna, Mae, put it: I never knew I could be free like that. Miraculously, I experience that facet of life at New Life For Girls I thought was inaccessible to me, the counseling dimension. I am no longer merely the transmitter of stories but have become a part of the New Life story. I pass through the looking glass. Rosa's way of ex-pressing it comes to mind: Through Wendy, and in such a tender way, God has exalted me.

AFTERWORD

At first, I misspelled the heading of this section: *Afterward*. It does seem that life after New Life has an altogether different quality and direction.

In my life after New Life, career no longer has the hold on my priorities and identity it once had. Not that I am passive. I completed my doctorate. I have continued to consult, began teaching an evening course in an MBA program, kept writing, and passed along this manuscript into that other wonderland, the world of publishing. My thoughts and prayers often turn to the women and men of New Life. I wonder how they are faring and whether I will see them again.

Gisetta keeps in touch via email. Several alumnae also stay in touch with me that way. Reunited with her sons, Gisetta tells me she works full time and is pleased to have an apartment and car. Holly and I saw each other at a subsequent New Life graduation. She works parttime and cares for her son. We exchanged phone numbers and made plans to meet at the fall ceremony, when Rosa was due to graduate.

Kenda married her fiancé. She returned to New Life for a month in 2003. Brooke worked with New Life in Westminster for several months after graduation. Tawanda returned to Chicago as she had planned, and married. In late 2004 she reentered New Life via the Westminster introduction center and now serves as a staff member.

Most of the staff members are still at New Life. Jade works fulltime for another Christian treatment program.

I asked the director about some of the other women who seemed to disappear. She responded gently: "Sometimes it is years before we hear from the women again. They get back in touch with us, eventually, when they're ready."

After Rosa's second return to New Life, I visited her at Dover a few times. We spent a happy afternoon together, ate lunch, stopped at a yard sale, and talked nonstop. In all the time she had spent at New Life—a total of thirty months—it was her first off-campus outing with a friend. She spent her free time with her mother and daughter. She spoke of her postgraduation plans to work in a ministry with her mother.

When I arrived at the October graduation, Hope was the first person I encountered. Beaming, she described her reunion with her children, her blossoming career at a nursing home, and her new townhome. Maria also works and lives with her children at a New Life center. Both women plan to continue their nursing education. Then I located Holly and Tawanda in the crowd.

Rosa graduated from New Life for Girls that night. Her teenaged daughter escorted her as she received her diploma. Hope, Tawanda, Holly, and I were there with hundreds of others to cheer her on.

Webster's dictionary defines "afterword" with this simple, enigmatic phrase: "epilogue 1." I had to use a magnifying glass to be sure the "1" was not a bracket. "Afterword" nests between "afterward" (" … thereafter") and "afterworld" (" … a world after death").

Yes, and I can live with that.

NOTES

Preface

Children's Bureau Adoption and Foster Care Analysis and Reporting System (AFCARS). Administration on Children, Youth and Families, U.S. Department of Health and Human Services, published March 31, 1999. Available: www.acf.dhhs.gov/programs/cb.

Chung, Connie (reporter/producer). *20/20 Special Report,* "Heroin Abuse in Communities," New York: ABC News, August 22, 2001.

"How Men and Women Enter Substance Abuse Treatment." *The Drug and Alcohol Services Information System (DASIS) Report,* Substance Abuse and Mental Health Services Administration (SAMHSA), U.S. Department of Health and Human Services, 2001.

McCaffrey, Barry R. "Treatment Protocol Effectiveness Survey." Treatment Outcome Working Group, United States Office of Drug Control Policy. Washington, D.C.: U.S. Printing Office, 1996.

Rodriguez, Cookie. *Please Make Me Cry!* Whitaker House, 1985.

Sacks, Oliver. *The Man Who Mistook His Wife for a Hat.* New York: Touchstone, 1998.

"Women in Substance Abuse Treatment." *The DASIS Report,* Substance Abuse and Mental Health Services Administration (SAMHSA), U.S. Department of Health and Human Services, 2001.

Introduction

www.newlifeforgirls.org

Part One

Carroll, Lewis. *Alice's Adventures in Wonderland and Through the Looking-Glass*. Barnes and Noble Classics, 2003.

Chapter 16

The theories about communities used in the exercises discussed in this chapter were culled from the following works:

Arensberg, C.M. and Kimball, S. T. *Culture and Community*. New York, Harcourt Brace & World, 1965.

Schein, E.H. *Organizational Culture and Leadership* (2nd Ed.). San Francisco: Jossey-Bass, 1992.

Chapter 19

Kilbourne, J. *Can't Buy My Love: How Advertising Changes the Way We Think and Feel* (originally published as: *Deadly Persuasion: Why Women and Girls Must Fight the Addictive Power of Advertising*). New York: Free Press, 1999. (**Author note:** a seminal work about the image of women in advertising.)

Pipher, M.B. *Reviving Ophelia: Saving the Selves of Adolescent Girls*. New York, Putnam, 1994. (**Author note:** a seminal work about the impact of U.S. culture on the identity formation and self-perception of teenaged girls.)

Chapter 20

Baker, M.M. *Community Building and the Power of Relationships in Organizations.* (Dissertation). Cincinnati: Union Institute and University, 2003.

Chapter 23

The "Jesus factor" studies mentioned in this chapter are three studies previous to my work that explore faith-based residential substance abuse treatment programs. All were conducted in the context of Teen Challenge programs and male alumni. They are:

Bicknese, D.A. *Comparison of Faith-based, STI and AA Drug Treatment Programs.* Evanston, IL: Northwestern University, 1999.

Hess, C.B. *Study of Teen Challenge Training Center* (demonstration project). Rehrersburg, PA: National Institute of Drug Abuse (NIDA), 1976.

Thompson, R.D. *Teen Challenge of Chattanooga, Tennessee Survey of Alumni.* (Simple, random-sample survey) Springfield, MO: Teen Challenge National, 1994.

For a bibliography of faith-based research studies, see also:

Johnson, B.R. Objective Hope: *Assessing the Effectiveness of Faith-based Organizations: A Review of the Literature.* Philadelphia: Center for Research on Religion and Urban Civil Society, 2002.

A chapter-by-chapter discussion guide for *Sandpaper Sisters* may be found at www.cultureconnects.com.

ABOUT THE AUTHOR

Michele McKnight Baker, Ph.D. is the founder and president of Culture Connects, providing organizational performance consulting services. She also founded Baker Marketing Communications, a corporate communications firm. Dr. Baker is a member of numerous professional and academic societies. She has served in various volunteer, leadership, and advisory roles with professional, community, and faith-based organizations.

Prior to founding her own company, Dr. Baker held executive management posts in California and Pennsylvania. Her writing has appeared in numerous regional and national publications. She serves as adjunct faculty and also speaks and presents seminars on a variety of business and marketing communications topics.

Dr. Baker is a graduate of Smith College and earned a Ph.D. in Organizational Studies from Union Institute and University. She serves in various leadership roles for professional and community organizations, including Rotary International.